Endorsements

Our country is desperate for someone to address what godly masculinity looks like. In this book, *Man UP*, my friend, Alex Bryant, examines the life of King David and shares insight that was passed along over 2,000 years ago to King Solomon the wisest man to have ever lived. This book was twenty years in the making as Alex lived out these principles and passed them along to his four boys. This book will help you become the man that God created you to be.

Mark Batterson
Lead pastor, National Community Church, Washington, D.C.
New York Times bestselling author of *Circle Maker*, *Win the Day* and others

Man UP is a book that we need right now. You don't have to look too hard to see that masculinity is being questioned and attacked all around us. Pastor Alex has been married to his childhood friend for nearly three decades and together they are raising four strong men and a little girl. He has lived the advice he is giving in this book. He uses humor and conversational style to engage the audience all throughout you won't want to put this book down.

Pastor Rich Wilkerson
Senior pastor Trinity Church, Miami, FL
Founder of Peacemakers

Learning from the life of King David, a man who was known for being after God's own hear, Alex offers insight into how God expects a man to act in this age of fatherless sons. This book is both funny and heart-warming. Man UP is a book that all men are guaranteed to learn from and enjoy.

Rob Ketterling
Lead pastor, River Valley Church, Savage, MN;
Author of *Change Before You Have To, Thrill Sequence, Front Row Leadership*, and others

This book was written by a MAN for MEN. Pastor Alex discusses all things that men relate to from sports to soldiers, great athletes to heroic warriors, handling money, being a father, and loving your woman. You'll experience his funny moments and things that touch your heart. No matter where you are in life, this book is for you.

Dick Hardy, Springfield, MO
Co-Founder of Leaders.Church

King David was a flawed man who lived a life with many ups and downs. At the end of his life, he left his son Solomon with words of wisdom that have stood the test of time. Pastor Alex has captured the heart of this advice in this book, Man Up. We are encouraged to be strong, obedient, and faithful so that we live the prosperous lives and be the men that God calls us to be. This book is a guide that will help you on your journey.

Jeff Leake
Lead pastor, Allison Park Church, Pittsburgh, PA
Author of *Praying with Confidence: 31 Days of Powerful Moments with God, God in Motion: Making Sense of the Loose Ends in Life*, and others.

The men of the Bible often challenged one another to step into the role of manhood. "Be a man" they encouraged one another. We still need that encouragement. With so much confusion around what it means to be a man, Alex offers clarity and a reminder it is still possible. Manhood is a responsibility we're called to take up. Alex will help you do it better. It's time to Man Up.

Chase Replogle
Pastor, Bent Oak Church, Springfield, MO
Author of *The 5 Masculine Instincts*

Man UP:
A Guide to Godly Masculinity

Man UP: a Guide to Godly Masculinity
Copyright 2023 by Alex Bryant. All rights reserved.

Published by Network 211 in partnership with
Three Clicks Publishing.

Scriptures marked NIV are taken from The Holy Bible, New International Version®, NIV® Copyright ©1973, 1978, 1984, 2011 by Biblica, Inc.® Used by permission. All rights reserved worldwide.

Scriptures marked KJV are taken from The Holy Bible, King James Version, public domain.

Scriptures marked ESV are taken from The Holy Bible, English Standard Version. ESV® Text Edition: 2016. Copyright © 2001 by Crossway Bibles, a publishing ministry of Good News Publishers.

Scriptures marked NLT are taken from The Holy Bible, New Living Translation, copyright ©1996, 2004, 2015 by Tyndale House Foundation. Used by permission of Tyndale House Publishers, Carol Stream, Illinois 60188. All rights reserved.

Scriptures marked NKJV are taken from The New King James Version®. Copyright © 1982 by Thomas Nelson. Used by permission. All rights reserved.

Scriptures marked CJB are taken from the Complete Jewish Bible, Copyright © 1998 by David H. Stern. All rights reserved.

The Holy Bible: New Century Version, containing the Old and New Testaments. 1991. Word Bibles: Dallas, TX.

NASB are taken from New American Standard Bible®, Copyright © 1960, 1971, 1977, 1995, 2020 by The Lockman Foundation. All rights reserved.

© 2023 by Alex Bryant. All rights reserved. No part of this book may be reproduced, stored in a retrieval system, or transmitted in any form or by any means–electronic, mechanical, photocopy, recording, or otherwise–without prior written permission of the copyright owner, except brief quotations used in connection with reviews in magazines or newspapers.

Interior template designed by Carrie Bywater;
Cover design by Christy Demoff

ISBN: 978-1-7355435-8-1
24 23 22 • 1 2 3

Printed in the United States of America

Man UP:
A Guide to Godly Masculinity

Alex Bryant

Three Clicks Publishing
Springfield, MO

First of all, I want to thank God for birthing this concept in my heart and mind all those years ago. I'm humbled that you continue to deem me worthy enough to use. Here I am Lord, use me.

To my family -Angela, Trey, Michael, Mason, Josh, and Katie -thanks for allowing me to share our stories. You are the best family a man could have. I love you all.

Thanks to Kevin and the team at Three Clicks Publishing for once again putting everything all together and bringing this book to the public.

This book has been 20+ years in the making and there are so many people who have been a part of making it happen. I mention many of you in this book but there are so many others who have played a role in my life and helped me to develop into the man I am today.

Thank you all.

Contents

Preface xii

Man UP Introduction xvii

Chapter 1: Man UP 1

Section 1: Be Strong Act Like A Man

Chapter 2: Don't Fear 11

Chapter 3: Don't Quit 23

Chapter 4: Demonstrate Excellence 35

Chapter 5: Team Work 45

Section 2: Be Observant Learn the Lord's Commands

Chapter 6: First Things First 57

Chapter 7: Daily Grind 69

Chapter 8: Discipline 83

Chapter 9: Sacrifice 97

Section 3: Be Faithful Walk in Obedience

Chapter 10: Anything is Possible 109

Chapter 11: Lock Your Family Up 121

Chapter 12: Daddying 133

Chapter13: Helping Others 153

Section 4: Endurance Keep Obeying

Chapter 14: Positive Thinking 167

Chapter 15: Learning From Others 181

Chapter 16: Continuous Improvement 195

Section 5: Prospering Obedience Brings Blessings

Chapter 17: Choices and Consequences 211

Chapter 18: Choose Joy 225

Chapter 19: God's Grace 241

Chapter 20: Get in Where You Fit In 255

Preface

I began writing this book nearly twenty years ago, after my second son was born. I had just turned 30, and the question popped into my head, "What would I want my boys to know if I wasn't around long enough to teach them to be men?" I'm naturally a list guy; lists excite me. Crossing things off my to-do list gives me great satisfaction. If I'm listening to a speaker who says he has a list of how to make my life better in any way, I grab my pen and composition notebook and get busy writing! Naturally, I decided to make a list for my boys. After mulling through my thirty years of life experience, I settled on sharing thirty nuggets of truth I had acquired. As I began to make my list and write down my thoughts, I decided to turn them into a book. I wondered who would want to read it but, I knew even if it were just for *my* boys, I would write a book. So I began. The words flowed easily. It turns out I had a lot to say.

I found it liberating to put my thoughts on a page. It was healing. It was motivating. As I began to share things I wanted my sons to know, it caused me to think about how I had learned the same truths. In the process, I came face to face with my past which gave me more to write about: the character and leadership traits of the men who taught me, the way they modeled things for me and didn't just tell me what I needed to know, the mistakes I made, and the ones I avoided by the grace of God.

God's timing always baffles me (until I get to the other side of a trial or project). The title for a book popped out at me early, but I sat on it for quite a while. While I waited, life kept going on all around me. My wife and I had three more kids to bring the total up to four boys and a girl. Then, from 2013 to 2015, I did inner-city ministry in St. Louis and realized that I had to get this message out not only for my sons but for men. Being a successful black man, I realized I could motivate other black men in ways I hadn't been encouraged as a young man. I wanted to address the specific challenges they face and inspire them to step their game up to be great husbands, fathers, and members of society. Around this time, I pitched the book to a few publishers who kindly rejected me. As a result, my insecurity increased, and I tabled the project. However, I did keep writing and blogging, and I actually published a different book with my wife, *Let's Start Again: A Biracial Couple's View on Race, Racial Ignorance, and Racial Insensitivity*. But I always knew I wanted to come back to this book, *Man UP*, and I kept asking the Lord for the right time to publish it.

Eventually, I realized that while I was waiting, I was growing. I was growing in my knowledge and understanding of what it takes to be a man and produce a man. Today, my oldest son is a senior in college and my second son a sophomore. My three other kids are now in high school and junior high. I'm not an expert, but I am extremely proud of who they are becoming, and I believe I have wisdom to share that can benefit other fathers. Some of my friends and mentees have told me I should write a book about this. Surprise! I already have. It's just a book no one has read before now because it's

Preface

been sitting on my shelf for twenty years. Of course, it is no surprise to God. Now I have more experience, knowledge, and wisdom. I can see the end of some of the stories that I shared, and I have earned a little credibility in this fatherhood business. The theories I have lived by have been tested and (by God's grace and to His glory) our kids have turned out very well. And although that little girl has upset the whole apple cart and caused me to change a lot of what I did with the boys in order to father her well, I'm managing. No, I'm thriving. I recently told my wife that I feel like I'm in the sweet spot of God. It's not because of me, definitely not. It's because of God's goodness and faithfulness and because I have done my best to live out what He has planted in my heart that I'm sharing with you in this book.

So here it is… *Man Up: A Guide to Godly Masculinity*. It's both new and improved and tried and true. It's a bit like a really good barbecue: it's been given time to marinate, and I pray it feeds your soul.

–Alex Bryant

Man **UP**: Introduction

By Alex Bryant

Society is experiencing a void. We lack men who are showing the next generation how to be strong and honorable, fulfilling responsibilities to family, community, and God. Many would say this is a new phenomenon, but I would argue this goes back to biblical times. The Bible is God's story. It describes His work to rescue rebels from their folly, guilt, and ruin. And in His rescue operation, God always takes the initiative.[1] In other words, the Bible is full of flawed men (and women) who encounter God's loving intervention on their life journey. This is good news because God's character is steadfast; it doesn't change. And He wants to intervene and rescue us, too.

As the thoughts and ideas for this book have been taking root in my heart and developing in my mind, I have been experiencing a time of deep reflection and intense learning. I have come to look at life and all its experiences as opportunities to learn and grow. I hope to impart the lessons I've learned to those who find this book in their hands.

One of my biggest motivations for penning these thoughts is that I want to instruct my children for the future. I am extremely blessed to have my family and they are my greatest earthly pleasure: my beautiful wife and best friend, Angela, and our five children.

---

1. Edmond Clowney, *The Unfolding Mystery, Discovering Christ in the Old Testament* (Presbyterian and Reformed, 1991), 89

I love my family. They are the family I've always wanted. When I was young, I always told people I was going to have all sons. The original plan was to have eleven boys, although I may not have mentioned that number to Ang. I wanted to coach my own football team–Bryant's BEARS! However, after Trey arrived and I saw how much energy it took to care for one, I lowered the number to five boys. Even though I was never a good basketball player, I figured I could learn to love the sport when all my boys would be running the pick and roll together. And they could still be the Bryant's Bears.

Mason Bryant inbounds the ball to Shaq Bryant (if I had another son, I would've named him Shaq. I'm not sure that my wife would approve, but just imagine with me for a moment!). Shaq dribbles it up the court (I know, but I said, use your imagination!) and passes it to Joshua Bryant. He dribbles to his left and then dishes it to Michael Bryant. Michael Bryant drives to the basket and throws up a floater to Trey Bryant, who is waiting for the alley-oop pass and slams it in for two points! The crowd goes wild as the Bryant boys win the state championship!

The point is...I always wanted all boys. I thought boys would be easier for me to handle, and after having four boys and then a little girl, I believe I was right. That little girl is a major handful! I can see you rolling your eyes right now. Admit it, you did. At the very least you smirked and thought to yourself: What does this guy know? What I know is that God had a different plan. He blessed me with four sons and

INTRODUCTION

a daughter, and I wouldn't change it for the world. (Did I mention my daughter plays basketball, too?) But seriously, I feel like I relate to boys well because of my personality. I tend to take the "toughen up" approach to life, and I want to teach my boys how to be MEN!

Another reason I'm compelled to write this book is because I believe there are a lot of men in the world who are still living like boys. I believe this book can offer them some important life lessons.

Here's where I give my view on the state of men in our society. These are generalizations, and like most generalizations, there are exceptions. Take time to think about what you are reading and write your reactions in the margins. You can even shoot me a note or an email about your thoughts if you'd like.

- Men are not taught to be men anymore. There are very few men even trying to teach these lessons! There are far too many fathers abandoning their children and leaving mothers to raise their sons by themselves.
- As a result, some men grow up trying to suppress their feelings and come across too "hard" or emotionally detached.
- Other men don't know how to be emotionally, mentally, and spiritually strong. They don't handle pressure well and tend to withdraw and not be effective leaders.
- Men in our society, particularly young men, lack the drive, discipline, determination, and motivation that previous generations had. Many of our fathers, grandfathers, and great-grandfathers had it rough growing up, and they had to learn how to make it. They faced adversity head on and became stronger men because of it.

- Men have become quick to avoid their responsibilities, choosing to focus on what makes them happy or what they think will help them become more successful. They don't want to accept blame or consequences for choices they make.
- Men make a lot of excuses for problems that come their way. They choose not to deal with problems. This pattern will eventually destroy them or at the least destroy their confidence and the confidence others have in them.
- Some men are unwilling or unable to make decisions. They lack the ability to "go for it." They allow fear and uncertainty to paralyze them.
- A lot of men are hardheaded and stubborn. They won't listen to wise counsel or accept good advice. Arrogance and pride block their ability to learn and grow.

Despite all this, I believe men are made in the image of God and have a divine call to be strong and courageous leaders for their families, communities, and the world. Yes, we have flaws and have failed in many ways, but there is time for us to step our game up and become the priests and kings God has called us to be. Men, strong godly men, are essential in fulfilling God's plan for this world. I am urged to shout from the rooftops. To all men, young and old, I say, "Man UP!" Listen, learn, be teachable, live with integrity, work hard, love, and serve like a man should. Man UP."

Chapter 1
Man UP

A number of years ago, I started on the journey of learning to become a man. I observed other men, both Christian and non-Christian, I read the Bible and other books, I listened to sermons, and I talked with other men. My goal was to learn to be the man that God had called me to be. I would love to proclaim that my journey is over. This isn't the case. The more I discovered about what it means to be a man, the more I realized that my journey would never end. So, I was faced with a choice: I could either decide that I didn't want to travel a never-ending road, or I could embrace the journey and learn as much as possible along the way. I chose the latter. So, this is the journey that I'm on, learning to be a man and how to Man UP.

Along the journey, my wife and I started our family. Now, in addition to learning to be a man myself, I realize I have the responsibility to teach my boys how to become men. More specifically, I need to teach them how to discover and become the kind of men God calls them to be. I want to teach my boys how to be men of God. I want them to learn what the Bible says about being a man, how they should act and speak, things they should avoid, and things they should regularly do. I want them to learn from my life. Some things I've learned the hard way and other things I was taught by mentors or other key men in my life. I want to show them how to act with integrity and assume responsibility for their actions. I want to teach them to live with honor and show respect for others. I want to teach them how to love: to love God with their whole heart, soul, and mind, and then to love other people as much as they love themselves. I want them to be teachable and willing to learn from anyone and everyone. I want them to know how to obey and serve. These principles are keys to being a leader, learning to obey directives, heed wise counsel, and serve those we lead. I want my boys to be better men than I am and avoid the mistakes I made. I want them to do more, go farther, be wiser, and love deeper than I have. I want them to Man UP.

OUR CASE STUDY: SOLOMON

One of the most compelling examples I can find of a father teaching his son to Man UP would be that of a Jewish king named David. David was the highly successful leader of the nation of Israel for many years. Although he made a lot of mistakes and did a lot of bad things, he had a good heart. In fact, the Bible tells us David was "a man after God's own heart."[2] As David was about to die, he realized he needed to pass on wisdom to his son, Solomon, who would succeed him as king. In 1 Kings 2:2-3 (NIV), David gave Solomon this charge:

"I am about to go the way of all the earth," he said. "So be strong, act like a man, and observe what the Lord your God requires: Walk in obedience to him, and keep his decrees and commands, his laws and regulations, as written in the Law of Moses. Do this so that you may prosper in all you do and wherever you go."

Manning Up has everything to do with knowing what God wants you to do and then doing it! This is what I want to teach my boys. Read the Bible to find out what God wants you to do. Study it, memorize it, meditate on it, read it again… and do what it tells you to do. Know it and then do it. Can it be that simple? Because if you learn to do this, as David told Solomon, you will be successful in everything you do. What a promise! What a blessing God offers to us. "Man UP and do what I tell you to do. Listen carefully and do everything, because when you obey me, I will bless you." WOW!

Fast-forward in the story of Solomon's life and notice his response. Solomon was as close to God as he was to his own father. He once had a conversation with God where God told him how pleased He was with him. In fact, God invited Solomon to request a special blessing from Him and promised He would fulfill the request. Solomon used divine wisdom to acknowledge his need for more wisdom. God granted this request and blessed Solomon, not only with increased

---
2. 1 Samuel 13:14, NIV.

wisdom and discernment, but also with great wealth, fame, and success.

Although Solomon had everything his heart could ever want or imagine including a close personal relationship with God and a life of service to Him, we find Solomon at a low point. Because of his love for women and his desire for pleasures of this world, he strayed from what he knew to be true and went on a search for human meaning and purpose. After years of public success and personal failure, he came to a conclusion that can change our lives. He determined that everything is meaningless. After all his wandering and searching with the advantage of God-given wisdom, Solomon's journey brought him back to the beginning of what his father taught him many years before. In Ecclesiastes 12:13-14 we read:

"Now all has been heard; here is the conclusion of the matter: Fear God and keep his commandments, for this is the whole duty of man. For God will bring every deed into judgment, including every hidden thing, whether it is good or evil."

"Man UP!" I charge you to listen, learn, be teachable, live with integrity, work hard, love, and serve like a man should. Young man–Man UP! Old man–Man UP! Learn from the teachings of David and the example of Solomon: read the Bible to find out God's plan and His will for your life. Study it, memorize it, meditate on it, read it again…and do what it tells you to do. In order to Man UP, you have to know God's Word and then have the fortitude to do what it says! I ask you again, can it be that simple? It can, and it is!

WHAT'S IN A NAME?

For a number of years, I contemplated the title of this book. More than once I settled on what I thought would be the official title. One name I strongly considered was *"Thirty Nuggets of Truth."* I love the thought of offering little pieces of advice that people can readily apply in their lives. I have always been the type of person who loves to learn, and I have had the wonderful privilege of learning from many wise people in my life. I strive to learn in all situations, whether the lessons come from my own experience, classroom learning, other people's mistakes–anywhere. I find it refreshing to know I have opportunities to grow in wisdom all the time. In this book, I hope to impart to you some of the nuggets of wisdom I have learned in my thirty-plus years of life on this earth.

Did you catch that? I had to call it "thirty-plus years" because I am (considerably) older than thirty years of age now. However, when I originally came up with the concept for this book, I was exactly thirty years old. Isn't it funny how it often takes us a while to complete the things the Lord lays on our heart? The Lord can make things happen instantly: just look at the work He performed at creation. With one word, He spoke the world into existence, and He can do the same thing again any time He chooses. The taking time part lies within us. It's a matter of God planting the seed of an idea deep in our hearts and nourishing it over time. It's also a matter of our taking time to become obedient to the point that we say, "Ok, Lord, I'm ready to do what you want me to do." When we get to this point, we are ready to move to the next level, allowing God to build courage within us to accomplish the task He has given us to do. I am reminded of how long it took Joshua to prepare when it was his time to replace Moses. God had him watch, learn, and train for over 40 years to get him ready to lead God's people. Forty years! It makes me feel better that it has "only" taken me about twenty years to complete this assignment from the Lord. Half the time it took Joshua, I might add. But I realize God's not finished with me, and I'm grateful for His abundant grace and patience.

I want this book to bless people. And although there are things everyone can relate to, I want to be clear: it's written from the perspective of a man, a Christian man, a black Christian man, a husband, a father, a son, a friend. That's what I am. These lessons are a collection of moments I have experienced in my life and the culmination of what I have learned through these experiences. I spend a lot of time working with students. To them, I am old. To others, I am young. It's a matter of perspective. And so is this book. In my first fifty years of life, God has shaped my perspective by allowing me to pick up a few nuggets of wisdom along the road. I share them with you. My goal is to improve the road I've traveled and make it better for those who come after me. To my boys, other young people who follow me, and anyone else who will listen, I offer these nuggets of truth and encouragement.

After this chapter, you will notice *Man UP* is organized into five sections, each containing a few chapters. I call it the 4+1 plan. The first four sections are a call to action for you. The final section is God's response. Here is an outline of the five sections:

- Section 1: Be Strong–Act Like a Man
- Section 2: Be Observant–Learn the Lord's Commands

- Section 3: Be Faithful–Walk in Obedience
- Section 4: Endure–Keep Obeying
- Section 5: Prosper–Obedience Brings Blessing

So, let's hit the road together. The plan is to make you laugh, maybe even cry a little, and definitely have you walk away wanting to be a better man. I've included all things man in this book: sports, fathering, business, mowing the lawn, soldiering, marriage, music, you name it. My prayer is that you enjoy reading this book as much as I loved writing it, and most of all that you apply it to the glory of God and the blessing of those in your life.

Section 1:
Be Strong
Act Like a Man

- Chapter 2 Don't Fear
- Chapter 3 Don't Quit
- Chapter 4 Demonstrate Excellence
- Chapter 5 Practice Teamwork

Chapter 2
Don't Fear

For God has not given us the spirit of fear, but of power and of love and of a sound mind.
—2 Timothy 1:7, NKJV

People seem to be full of fear these days. From the fear of dying and the fear of heights, to the fear of public speaking, people are being paralyzed by their phobias. I did a quick Google search and here's what they list as the top-five phobias.

1. Claustrophobia: The fear of tight spaces.
2. Social Phobia: The fear of judgment or rejection.
3. Arachnophobia: The fear of spiders.
4. Acrophobia: The fear of heights.
5. Agoraphobia: The fear of open or crowded spaces.

Do you identify with any of those? I'll admit, this brotha is irrationally afraid of heights. Ang and I took an anniversary trip to Vegas once and she talked me into going on the high roller Ferris Wheel. I thought I was going to die. As the 45-minute journey rotated up to 18 stories high, I sat there staring at the ground. Ang and the 25 other daredevil tourists in our pod were walking all around looking at the Vegas skyline, taking pictures, and enjoying the view. The whole time I just sat there clinging to the bench I was on, staring downward, not talking, and definitely not moving. I literally could not move. I'm sure that was a funny sight for the other passengers to see a 300-pound, big, bald, black dude cower in the corner. Looking back, I'll admit it wasn't my finest moment, but I wasn't embarrassed in the least. I was too worried about falling to my death.

Aside from that incident, I think others will agree I'm usually known for being a courageous guy. One part of being strong is learning to live without or beyond fear. In our featured text, we see King David wanted to be certain his son, Solomon, understood this before he succeeded David to the throne.

David faced danger many times in his life. In the end, he was known as a brave and valiant man. He never balked in the face of danger, starting at a young age. While working as a shepherd boy in his father's field he faced danger when both a lion and bear tried to harm the flock.[3] In fact, Scripture reveals that not only did he not cower, but he went after the lion and the bear, seizing them by the fur, and killed them in order to protect the flock. As a young man, he faced danger head on when he opposed Goliath, the nine-foot-tall Philistine who was threatening God's people. Scripture reveals David ran quickly toward the battle line to meet Goliath.[4] That's

---
3. 1 Samuel 17:34-37, NIV.
4. 1 Samuel 17:48, NIV.

taking courage to a whole other level–running towards the giant!

Those aren't the only examples of David not shrinking back in the face of fear. When the mad and delusional King Saul hunted him and tried to take his life, David repeatedly eluded him without showing fear. In the midst of all the danger that surrounded his life, David learned to live without and beyond fear. David faced lions, bears, and madmen (oh my!). These should provoke some degree of fear. Yet David learned to be bold and courageous. He didn't let the fear control him or paralyze him. Instead, he controlled the fear. He confronted it and was victorious over it. David knew Solomon would need to learn to do the same in order to become the king that his father thought he could become. David wanted to ensure that Solomon understood that being strong meant he would have to learn to overcome fear.

THE SIGNS ARE CLEAR

I remember reading a sign on a billboard one time that asked the question, "What would you attempt to accomplish for God if you knew you couldn't fail?" That got me thinking about courage and led me to ask myself a few questions that I submit to you now. If failure wasn't an option, what would you try to do for the Lord? What task or project would you undertake? What business or community organization would you start if you knew it was going to be a success? Who would you share Jesus with? What career would you select? What would you do for Jesus if you knew from the beginning that He would bless your endeavor and it would succeed? That billboard got me thinking about all the things

I wanted to accomplish for the Lord but was a little unsure about. It made me reconsider the goals and dreams He had placed in my heart that I had not attempted because I was afraid of failing.

UNLOCKING YOUR POTENTIAL

I've read the average person only reaches about 15 percent of their potential in their lifetime. It's sad to think we're leaving all that potential success on the table. And how many are living lives without any recognized meaning or purpose? If 15 percent is the average, think how many aren't even hitting that low bar. This means that most of the goals and dreams people have in their hearts and minds from their youth, don't usually come to pass. Not because we're incapable of achieving them, but because we don't do what is possible to make it happen. That's amazing.

Initially I thought about the actual percentage itself. I mean, who comes up with this stuff and how do they measure it? And who are the "they" doing this research and sharing this statistic? I have heard it jokingly said that 80 percent of all statistics are made up. I appreciate the irony in that statement. Yet, for a moment, let's assume that the statistic about people reaching their full potential is wrong. What if people tend to reach more than 15 percent of their full potential? What if they double the reported statistic and reach 30 percent of their full potential? What if they accomplish half the things they want to in their lifetime? The fact still remains: people are not fulfilling all that God intended or has made possible. What about you? How close are you to accomplishing all that God wants you to accomplish? And you may be thinking I'm not done yet. I still have time. Maybe so, but what are the things God has placed on your heart and prodded your spirit to do that you have yet to begin?

Most of us won't accomplish all that God wants or intends for us to accomplish in our lifetimes. You know it's true. Think about all the bright ideas that pop into your head on a regular basis. Somehow the natural routine of life allows those ideas to fade like the sunset at the end of the day. And what started as a bright idea quickly dims until its light is no more. Many of them we will never think about again. The potential is lost, and we let it happen.

What about all the plans you make? When some of your bright ideas actually advance into the planning stage, you have every good intention of doing something great with that idea. But then, something happens. You lose sight of the idea, it's replaced by busyness or competing priorities, and it is relegated to that the list of things we plan on getting to someday. Sadly, that someday usually never comes. The reality is that your idea never really made it into a true planning stage. It was something you wished you would get around to. And I've learned a goal without a plan, is just a wish.

The saddest of all these lost potential situations are the ones we don't even attempt to accomplish because of fear. It may be fear of failure, fear of the unknown, or fear of the pressure that might ensue by taking a chance to do something. For whatever reason, a lot of us don't even try. This is a shame! In his book, *Chase the Lion,* author and pastor Mark Batterson compels us to quit playing it safe and start running toward the roar![5] That's what King David did, he ran towards the roar of the lion, the bear, and even the giant, Goliath. We need more men who will determine that they will not fear, and instead Man UP. They need to run forward with courage instead of being paralyzed by fear.

TWO PLANS FOR YOUR LIFE

It's time to realize that Satan has a plan for your life. He uses tactics like fear, busyness, other obligations, and our perceived lack of resources, to stop us from accomplishing the things God intended for us to do. He wants to hinder us and paralyze us, and he will employ any means necessary to accomplish his goal. The enemy knows if he can slow you down long enough, your destined accomplishments will turn into lost potential. Brothers, we must not allow this to happen.

God has a plan for your life, too. And He offers resources and strategies to empower us to accomplish His plan. He offers us a spirit of power, love, and a sound mind. The Bible says clearly in 2 Timothy 1:7 that "God has not given us the spirit of fear but of power and of love and of a sound mind." Some translations say God has not given us the spirit of *"timidity"*[6]. God doesn't want us to be timid in our actions. When He gives us something to do, He wants us to walk in boldness while attempting to accomplish the task. I will add that He intends for us to use wisdom while planning for the task. Colossians 4:5 tells us to *"be wise in the way you act, making the most of every opportunity."*[7] God expects us to

---
5. Mark Batterson. *Chase the Lion: If Your Dream Doesn't Scare You, It's Too Small.* (Colorado Springs, CO: Multnomah, 2016).
6. New Living and New American Standard Translations.
7. Colossians 4:5, NIV.

work vigorously while performing the tasks He sets before us. His Word teaches us that in all we do, He requires us to be relentless in completing the task, working at it with all our heart, as if we are working for the Lord.[8]

When we do our part, He will give us His own power to ensure we are successful in our work for Him. It's amazing that God offers you and I His power. Can you believe that? This is the same power that enabled Peter to walk on water, and the same power that raised Lazarus from the dead. It's supernaturally charged and sent directly to you and me on earth. This power accomplishes great things and small things. It's the power that allowed David to face Goliath and walk away victorious. The same power gave Paul the boldness to preach the gospel all over Asia and helped him convert people to become followers of Christ after he spent years persecuting and killing Christians. This is the very same power that Christ used to conquer the grave, and if you have accepted Christ as your savior, it lives inside of you.[9] God's Spirit of power offers us courage to face the challenges that lie ahead with confidence, knowing that our God is with us and for us, He's working in us and through us, and what He wants to happen will happen.

Another gift God offers us is the ability to love others as well as we love ourselves. His Spirit allows us to look past offenses and not be easily offended by others. We don't have to return the hate and vitriol others spew at us. This spirit of love allows us to live in peace and harmony with our fellow man, no matter their race or color, age, belief system, or

---

8. Colossians 3:23, NIV.
9. Romans 8:11, NLT, "The Spirit of God, who raised Jesus from the dead, lives in you."

political affiliation. God enables us to keep moving forward when others ridicule us and persecute us in the midst of our journey. This is the same spirit of love that allowed heroes of the faith, like Joseph, to shake off the offense of his brothers selling him into slavery and separating him from his family. Joseph didn't know that overcoming this trial would allow him to later go on and save his family and many others. This kind of love allows us to press on and not stop in the face of opposition or persecution. Proverbs 17:9 says: *"He who covers over an offense promotes love."* God gives us this love.

God also gives us the spirit of a sound mind.[10] Some translations say a spirit of self-control or discipline.[11] God wants us to have discipline in the way we live our lives. He expects us to be self-controlled in all areas. Proverbs 6 talks about things the Lord hates: proud eyes, a lying tongue, murder, minds that think up evil schemes, feet that are quick to do evil, a false witness, those who stir up dissension.[12] If God hates these things, we need to use self-control in avoiding them. When we display self-discipline, we prove ourselves to be faithful, trustworthy servants. It is this type of servant God chooses to utilize in accomplishing great things for His kingdom. When we demonstrate this type of self-control and discipline, we are saying to God with our actions that we want to accomplish something for Him. It is at this point that we can walk forward without fear knowing He is on our side. When God is for you, who can be against you?![13]

---

10. 2 Timothy 1:7, KJV.
11. 2 Timothy 1:7, ESV and NLT.
12. Proverbs 6:16-19, NIV.
13. Romans 8:31, KJV.

REMAIN IN HIM

A while ago I received a revelation from God. I was thinking about all the things I wanted to accomplish for Him, all the goals and dreams that were in my heart. Side note, like many others, I have wrestled with the question of how I know if the things I want to accomplish are from God or from myself. I admit I often struggle with recognizing the difference. I have a lot of ideas that pop into my head; some of them fade away fairly quickly. This can be a good thing, because not all my ideas are winners. That being said, sometimes I find myself waiting or hesitating to move forward with an idea while I try to discern if it's from the Lord or not. I mean how do I really know if it's a **God idea**? The revelation I received from God is this:

If I remain true to God and show myself to be a faithful servant, I will accomplish everything that He has for me to do in my lifetime, nothing more and nothing less.

I have found this revelation to be very comforting and reassuring. All I have to do is remain true to God, and never walk outside of His will. I am called to remain true to my faith and not waiver. This is what it means to show my faithfulness to God. My faithfulness shows I am a trustworthy and available servant who is willing and available for Him to use however and whenever He chooses. When I do my part, God will take care of the rest. I'm humbled to know when I'm obedient God will ensure I achieve the things He has in life for me to achieve. My success is no longer for me to worry about because it's up to Him to empower me to be successful and reach my full potential. It's a blessing to know that God has my back!

The word that God gave me applies to you as well, my friend. If you remain faithful and obedient, you will accomplish all that He has for you to accomplish in life, nothing more and nothing less! Allow this to give you courage to be strong, and to reject fear from paralyzing you from taking action. Fear of failure, fear of the unknown, fear of losing control - none of these are from the Lord. He's not the one who gives us the spirit of fear.

Remember that success comes from the Lord. Achievement and accomplishments all come from the Lord. So, don't fear. God has your back. His word teaches us that He will give us all we need in order to accomplish all He has called us to do. This is the meaning of Romans 8:28, when Paul taught us "All things work together for good to them that love God, to them who are called according to his purpose." This should give you the peace of mind and the courage of heart to Man UP and set out to accomplish all God has placed in your heart to do for Him. Don't allow fear to be the thing that prevents you from experiencing all the great things He has in store for you. Remember, like Wayne Gretzky said, you miss 100 percent of the shots you don't take. You miss out on all opportunities that you let pass. You fail every test that you avoid. You can't win unless you are willing to get off the bench and get in the game. So, take a few shots and see what happens. Maybe God will act on your behalf. Nothing can stop the Lord from doing what He wants to do, whether by many or by few.[14] So, Man

---

14. 1 Samuel 14:6 (NIV) "Jonathan said to his young armor-bearer, "Come, let's go over to the outpost of those uncircumcised men. Perhaps the LORD will act on our behalf. Nothing can hinder the LORD from saving, whether by many or by few."

Don't Fear

Up and remain in Him, stay faithful and true and remember God has your back.

Chapter 3
Don't Quit

**Winners never quit.
Quitters never win!
–Vince Lombardi**

I like people who win! Being that I'm a huge fan, when I think of winners, a few people instantly come to mind. People like Jerry Rice, the greatest wide receiver of all time who won three Super Bowls with the 49ers and was a two-time Super Bowl MVP. Winners like Walter Payton, my favorite Chicago Bear of all time, who held the NFL record for most career yards for a number of years. Sweetness did the Super Bowl Shuffle on his way to winning Super Bowl XX (that's 20 for those who aren't familiar with Roman numerals) with the 1985 Chicago Bears. Another great winner is Mohammad Ali, three-time heavyweight champion of the world. Like me, many believe he is the greatest boxer of all time. Because of their flaws I don't know if it's still acceptable to admit that I still like Lance Armstrong, winner of seven Tour de France races, and Barry Bonds, the MLB all-time home run leader. Bonds definitely belongs in the Hall of Fame, by the way. Outside of sports there are other winners that I admire, people like Sam Walton, Bill Gates, Elon Musk, and Warren Buffet. All of these people have proven that they are leaders and industry winners in their prospective areas of expertise. They have stood in the face of adversity and come out victorious. There are so many others, but these are a few of my favorites.

I have always admired people who like to win. Most people will say they want to win, but they are not really willing to give what it takes to be a winner. They may talk about winning, they might even give it the "good ole' college try," but when it's all said and done, they falter in the face of adversity. They fold when the going gets tough. They give up when things get too hard. They quit.

BE STRONG! DON'T BE A QUITTER! MAN UP!

As a lifelong diehard Chicago Bears fan, I don't like anything about the Green Bay Packers, so it was hard for me to even include this saying by their legendary coach Vince Lombardi. However, it embodies everything I believe in life when it comes to Manning UP and being strong. Lombardi said, **"Winners never quit, and quitters never win!"** He went on to say a very common-sense statement that I'm afraid many have forgotten in our society. He said, "If it doesn't matter who wins or loses, then why do they keep score?"[15]

---
15. https://www.brainyquote.com/quotes/vince_lombardi_100525

I've come to realize that whether we like it or not, score is being kept in the game of life.

The Bible teaches us to endure through hardship and to finish each race strong. We are encouraged to persevere and not quit. *If you give up when trouble comes, it shows that you are weak*[16]. Take the time to stop and think about this statement and evaluate yourself. Are you the type of person who gives up when trouble comes? What does this say about you? If you quit when things get tough, are you manning UP? Of course not! As a husband, father, community member, and small business owner, I admit life can be extremely difficult. There are so many demands pulling at men today. Financial demands to be a provider for your family, social demands for your time and energy, physical demands for you to be present and protect your family in this crazy world. I get it. There is a lot pulling at us, trying to wear us down and get us to tap out. Don't do it, though! Real men don't quit even when things are tough, when things aren't going their way, and when the outcome doesn't look so good.

INTEGRITY

Enduring and hanging in there speaks volumes about a man's integrity. This is one of the main ingredients required to be strong and Man UP. Real men are people of integrity. Integrity can be defined as:

1. Always telling the truth.
2. Doing what you say you will do.
3. Accepting responsibility for your actions.[17]

---
16. Proverbs 24:10, NCV.
17. Ross Campbell, *Help Your Twenty-Something Get a Life and Get it Now* (Nashville, TN: Thomas Nelson, 2007).

Winning and quitting both have to do with integrity. Winners are people of integrity. They are truthful and honest in their pursuit of success. They don't cheat or cut corners. They are not the kind of people who avoid getting caught cheating. Instead, they choose not to cheat. They do what they say they will do by striving hard to keep their commitments. Even when the outcome isn't what they want, winners accept responsibility for their actions.

Quitters, on the other hand, are much different. Many quitters lack integrity, and it stands out to others around them. They are usually willing to cheat or cut corners if they believe it will help them get ahead. They are often the type of people who play dirty and are known for giving up easily. Quitters usually lack discipline in their personal lives and make a habit of not doing what they say they will do. They look to blame anyone but themselves for the failures they experience. It's hard to respect quitters.

> **The man of integrity walks securely,**
> **But he who takes crooked paths will be found out.**
> **–Provers 10:9**

Winners are the type of people who play with integrity all the time. Most of the time they find themselves on top of the scoreboard as well, but this isn't always the case. Although winners want to finish each endeavor on the top, they are not willing to compromise in order to get there. It's true that the scoreboard determines who ultimately wins and who loses. Real winners are willing to accept temporary setbacks and work harder to finish on top the next time. They are resilient!

They realize that winning is not something that happens to them, it's something they learn to do. A few days ago, I saw a man wearing a t-shirt that spoke to this. In big letters it said, "I never lose." In small letters, it said, "I either win or I learn." That's a winner mentality!

I've learned that winning is the result of a series of positive and good choices. Winners are willing to do what it takes to live with integrity–they either win or they learn. As a result, they usually find security in their lives. They do what is right and consistently give their best effort, realizing their integrity cannot always be accurately determined by or displayed on a scoreboard.

On the other hand, quitters only want to see themselves on top. They are willing to lie, cheat, and steal in order to get there. When they realize they may not win, they give up, avoiding the embarrassment of losing. This allows them to say they didn't really try because they didn't really care anyway. Have you been around people like this? They want to win so badly, and they can't stand the thought of not finishing on top. They would rather quit.

I've seen this pattern start with people on the athletic field, and carry over into other arenas of their life. Instead of giving their all at work and learning to be a better employee, they would rather quit and declare they didn't want to work there anyway, or the boss was a jerk, or they were wronged somehow by their coworkers. Instead of working through difficult times in their relationships, they emotionally check out and walk away, looking for a more shallow relationship where they can start anew. They would rather cut tail and run instead of Manning UP and working through difficult times.

PUT SOME RESPECT ON MY NAME

When my oldest son Trey was seven years old, we got him the game Disney Pixar Monopoly for his birthday. He absolutely loved playing that game, so literally every day for the first three weeks, someone in the family played with him. He started to get pretty good at the game and would let anyone who would listen know he was undefeated against his brother Michael. This was no great feat considering Michael was only 4 years old and could barely count to twenty by himself.

Nonetheless, Trey made it known he was on a winning streak. It was funny that he counted these games as a victory because most of the time Michael would get bored after about 30 minutes and walk away from the table; he was more interested in playing with his Lightning McQueen car. Yet, Trey counted this as a "W" nonetheless. I would have, too. Michael wasn't the only regular victim, however. Trey would often beat his mom who doesn't have a natural killer instinct when it comes to playing games, like the rest of us in the Bryant family. She plays games for the fun of it and enjoys the family time over the competition aspect. Although my wife has a competitive side that usually shows itself when she competes against me, she couldn't bring herself to take her seven-year-old son as a serious competitor. As a result, Trey beat her several times early on. To this day, I don't know that Ang has ever beat Trey at Monopoly, and she's okay with that.

The last of Trey's victims during this time were his grandma and grandpa. My stepdad, Mike, was the only father I ever knew so I will honor him by referring to him as my dad for the rest of this book. At that time, he and my mom lived with us for a few months, and they were usually available to play with their first grandson. My dad was a serious competitor who regularly won most of the games he played with me when I was younger. However, something was different with Trey. Maybe he got soft or wasn't as sharp in his old age, because Trey would lay the smack down on both grandparents every now and then. I'm certain they were trying hard and played to win, but it was obvious that Trey was pretty good.

That is until it came to playing me. Now, I'm not the kind of dad that is prone to letting kids win games, especially one as serious as Monopoly. Don't get me wrong, when playing basketball, I would let them score every now and then, or when racing, give them a head start to make it competitive, but my kids know, they better think long and hard if they expect me to roll over and let them WIN! You gotta' be kidding me! Nah bruh, nah! You best believe that even when playing Monopoly against my own boy, I play to win.

It bothered Trey that he could beat everyone else in the house at one time or another except me. He got very upset and decided that he didn't want to play me anymore until he got a little better. In consulting with his grandma about my competitive nature, she informed him that I had always been the type who plays to win, no matter what it is. She told him the story about when I got in trouble with her because I refused to let my younger sister win a game. She wanted me to help build my sister's confidence and let her win a game, but I just couldn't stand to lose! I opted to get punished rather than throw the game. While I'd like to say that was a reflection of my integrity from an early age, it was a greater reflection of how competitive I was, and really, still am. This made Trey desire to beat me even more.

Finally, after a month of practice, he laid down the challenge–old buck vs. young buck, father vs. son, youth vs. wisdom. He was ready to try to take my Monopoly family title. We laid the board out and began to play, and it quickly became evident that he had improved. Trey had learned to strategize, and he was a pretty good Monopoly player, especially for his age. The game went back and forth for a good while with each of us owning key properties with Al's Toy Barns on them (these would be considered hotels in the original Monopoly). Even though there was no clear winner, Ang was calling for me to end the game because it was a school night and well past Trey's bedtime. But how could I? I mean sometimes a man's gotta do what a man's gotta do and at this time, I had to lay the smack down on my seven-year-old son who was trying to take my title. Bedtime, rest, and school–they all could wait!

It was a hard-fought battle, but in the end, I was able to hold him off and win the game. Trey was upset and disappointed and began to cry. He was so furious that he didn't want to shake my hand. He was mad at me because he thought he was going to win, but I ended up beating him. He wanted nothing to do with me, and Ang had to come in and help console him. In a normal situation like this where I made an opponent cry, I would be tempted to gloat and rub it in even more. But this was my own little boy. And seeing him hurt diminished the sweetness of my victory.

THE LESSON TO BE LEARNED

Recognizing this was a teaching moment, after I gave him a moment to cool off, I took him in my arms and gave him the talk. I let him know I was proud of him for the effort he gave. I told him he played a good game and showed himself to be a clever and mature Monopoly player and he should be proud of that. I gave him props for giving me a run for my money. And I let him know I was the one who ended victorious that day. But I didn't say it to rub it in. I explained to him that part of becoming a good winner is learning to lose graciously, and then you come back to fight another day. With tears rolling down his face, I asked him if he understood. He shook his head yes and wiped away his tears. I told him I loved him, and I had a lot of respect for him. I let him know I was honored to play such a worthy opponent. I assured him he had nothing to be ashamed of and he should hold his head high.

My son learned a valuable lesson that day: Just because you lose a game doesn't mean you are a loser. Learn from the loss and come back and play harder the next time. I was thankful for this opportunity to teach my boy a life lesson. Years later, I can tell you that talk worked. Our family loves to play cards and board games, and Trey is now an excellent Monopoly player. He's very competitive and can always find a way to challenge for the top spot. He has had his share of victories during our family games. Although, let's be honest, I'm still the top dog in my house! Yet, I have no doubt that Trey and all the rest of our kids will be winners in life. They have learned to play hard, are very smart, know how to strategize, give maximum effort in all they do, don't like to lose, and never quit. They have learned to be winners and have the tools necessary to ensure success. I'm excited to see what they do in the future.

BECOMING A WINNER

What about you? Are you a winner? Are you on the road to becoming a winner? In order to be the winner that you were created to be, I encourage you to adopt the following actions steps:

1. **Don't look for the easy way out.** Avoid taking shortcuts in life. If you find yourself willing to cut corners or take the easy way out when things get hard, you will end up quitting. Make winning a habit and remember, the little things matter.

2. **Be determined.** Things will get tough because life is hard and problems are inevitable. Be ready for them so you are not caught off guard. Boxers will tell you the knockout blow is the one you don't see coming. Be always ready, and be determined that when the problems come, you will fight through them.

3. **Focus on the long term instead of the short term.** Most people quit because they don't see the light at the end of the tunnel. They give up hope. When they don't see a path to victory, they think they might as well give up. Don't quit! Keep your eyes on the big picture and it will help you endure.

4. **Work hard and focus on the prize you are striving to acquire.** Be the type of person who gives their best effort. Don't just bide your time and hope you win. Try hard, work for it, and keep your eye on the prize! To the victor go the spoils. The hero gets the girl!

Don't Quit

It's important to learn to be a winner in the small things in life so that you learn to be a winner in the most important thing in life. The most important competition we are all involved in is the one for our souls. You can't cheat in this life race, and if you quit you will not receive the reward. In fact, you will be punished for quitting this race, and it will be the worst punishment you can imagine. But if you endure and do not quit, you will win. The Bible says:

I have fought the good fight, I have finished the race, I have kept the faith. Now, a crown is being held for me–a crown for being right with God. The Lord, the judge who judges rightly, will give the crown to me on that day - and not only to me but to all those who have waited with love for him to come again.[18]

This is an encouragement for all of us to endure until the day Christ will come to judge all people and take His people to live with Him in heaven. You can't get there by giving up or quitting in the game of life.

The bottom line is this: if you want to win at life and spend eternity in heaven, you need to Man UP! Work on your mental, emotional, and spiritual strength so that you are strong enough to endure to the end. Be determined not to quit when things get hard or when the road gets tough. It may take time to develop this habit in your life, but it will be worth the work.

FIND STRENGTH IN THE LORD

We learn a great lesson from King David in 1 Samuel 30. After returning from battle, David and his men found their

---
18. 2 Timothy 4:7–8, NCV.

camp had been raided and their wives and children had been carried off as captives. David's men were so angry at his leadership that they were ready to kill him. The Bible says that David was greatly distressed because his men wanted to stone him. That would be a terrible way to die! David could have easily felt sorry for himself, given up hope, and decided to quit. I'm sure he may have felt like giving up since he lost his family and now his men were turning against him. However, instead of giving up hope and throwing in the towel, David showed us what to do in hard situations. Instead of giving up hope, David encouraged himself in the LORD his God.[19] Other translations say, "David strengthened himself in the LORD"[20]

Can I encourage you that instead of giving up and quitting when things get hard, Man UP and strengthen yourself in the Lord. That's where you will find a never-ending source of strength to be the man that God has called you to be.

---

19. 1 Samuel 30:6, KJV.
20. 1 Samuel 30:6, ESV and NKJV.

Chapter 4
Demonstrate Excellence

If you don't have time to do it right the first time, will you have time to do it over?

From the time I was physically able to push a lawn mower in somewhat of a straight line, I had the responsibility of mowing our lawn every Saturday morning. Since my dad was old school, I didn't get paid for this job either. It was a chore that I was expected to do every week in exchange for room and board. My dad was a no-nonsense kind of guy. When he said something, he meant it. When he told me to do something, he expected it to be done right then. He made it clear that no matter how late I stayed out on Friday night, he expected the lawn to be mowed first thing Saturday morning, and he wanted it to be done the way he had shown me to do it. My dad made it clear to me that the proper maintenance of our small, humble yard was my sole purpose for living.

He trained me to think about what I was doing and to do it to the best of my ability. He didn't want me to just push the mower over the grass and hope I cut most of it. I was to mow in straight lines and make sure I didn't miss any spots. He wanted the edges trimmed properly and looking straight and sharp. Because we couldn't afford a weed eater, this was no small task. I'm reasonably certain I'm the last person on the planet to use the old-fashioned hand trimmers. For those of you who don't even know what I'm talking about, hand trimmers were basically oversized, outdoor scissors that required getting down on the ground and cutting a few blades of grass at a time. My dad wanted me to take pride in the job I was doing, even though it seemed like an unimportant weekly chore.

DEFINING SUCCESS

Early on, before I proved myself to be a quality craftsman, he would walk around and inspect my work when I was finished. There were a few times when I tried to cut corners and not do my best work because I was in a hurry to get done and go play ball. My dad knew what was up and if I left without telling him, I had to deal with his wrath when I returned.

While he appeared to be checking my work, he was also teaching me what success was. Whether it's mowing the lawn, having a good marriage, or raising independent kids, we must learn what success looks like. And invariably, it looks like hard work.

Demonstrate Excellence

The greatest coach of all time, John Wooden, said, "Success is peace of mind that is a direct result of self-satisfaction in knowing you did your best to become the best you are capable of becoming."[21] Wooden believed that although our reputation is important, our character is even more important. We are the only ones who really know the truth about our own capabilities and performance. To continually improve and work to be a strong successful man, Wooden suggests we ask ourselves two questions: 1) Did we do our best at this point in our life? and 2) Did we leave it all on the field, in the classroom, at the office, or in the trenches? If we can say we did, then we are a success in that situation and at that stage in life.

More simply put, success means doing the best we can with what we have. We achieve success in learning from and growing through what we do, not from what we ultimately accomplish. Don't get me wrong, my dad expected the yard to look nice, but more than that he was teaching me to have high personal standards and to always strive for exceptional performance. I didn't recognize it then, but it's clear to me now.

Motivational speaker and best-selling author Zig Ziglar said that success is achieving the best version of yourself. He taught that success is a journey rather than a destination. He said, "There is no finish line to your success, it is a continual process of self-improvement."[22]

My dad wasn't mean. For the most part, he was very kind and patient. And although he wasn't highly educated, he was

---

21. John Wooden and Jay Carty. *Pyramid of Success: Building Block for a Better Life.* (Ventura, CA: Regal Books, 2005).
22. https://www.ziglar.com/

intelligent and wise. He knew it was important to teach me how to develop a good work ethic. He grew up in the generation where it was the norm for people to work hard to get ahead. Working hard was just the right thing to do. He told me that as a black man, I needed to make sure I earned a reputation for being a hard worker. He explained things wouldn't come easy for me, and I would need to work for everything I got in life. Many of these sayings may be considered "cliché," but they have been proven true time and again.

TIMELESS TRUTHS LEARNED IN AN UNCOMMON WAY

Although he never referenced them by name, my father taught me timeless principles from men like George Washington Carver, who taught there is no shortcut to achievement. Carver believed that we should learn to do common things uncommonly well.[23] Booker T. Washington echoed this sentiment when defining excellence as doing uncommon things in an uncommon way.[24] By showing me how to mow the lawn and then giving me the opportunity to do it myself, my dad was teaching me responsibility. I believe the key to my learning how to complete tasks the right way was in his inspections. Dad would give specific and direct feedback to critique and guide me. He wanted me to take pride in the job I was doing, even though it seemed insignificant to me. The yard needed to be mowed, and I could learn to be a hard worker at the same time. It wasn't until much later in life

---

23. Sam Wellman, *George Washington Carver: Inventor and Naturalist*. (Uhrichsville, OH: Barbour Publishing), 1998.
24. Alan Schroeder, *Booker T. Washington: Educator and Spokesman*. (New York: Chelsea House Publications), 1992.

that I realized the education my dad was giving me was far more valuable than any allowance he could have dished out– although I would have appreciated both. W. E. B Dubois said, "The return from your work must be the satisfaction which that work brings you and the world's need of that work."[25] I don't remember my dad ever reading Dubois, but he passed that lesson down to me loud and clear.

As I've gotten older, I've come to realize the value of doing things with excellence. This concept is hard for many younger people to grasp, because they tend to think about the extra time it will take to do things better than if they give the minimal effort. But excellence can't be measured up front based on the time required to a finish a task. Excellence can't be fully recognized until the back end. My experiences in life have helped me realize that part of being a strong man is developing the reputation for excellence, for being a person of high character. And high character doesn't cut corners; it commits to the standard no matter how long it takes to get there.

DEFINITION OF EXCELLENCE

I want to encourage you to be a strong man who strives for excellence in everything you do. I'm told this is part of the Air Force Core Values: Integrity First, Service Before Self, and Excellence in All We Do. The Bible teaches that whatever work you do, do your best, because you are going to the grave, where there is no working, no planning, no knowledge, and no wisdom.[26] The actual phrase it uses is, "Whatever your

---

25. http://duboiscenter.library.umass.edu/du-bois-quotes/
26. Ecclesiastes 9:10, paraphrase.

hand finds to do, do it with all your might." Why? Because life is short, and you won't be able to do things differently when you are dead. You might as well do things right now, while you are able.

Legendary basketball coach, Pat Riley, defines excellence as "the gradual result of always striving to be better."[27] That's the deal. Be committed to continually growing and striving to get a little better all the time. You may not be good at a particular task or skill right now. You may be average a little below average. Work to improve. After you consistently put in the time, you will see the progress as you move closer to where you want to be.

Consistency is key. Philosopher Will Durant, said, "We are what we repeatedly do. Excellence, then, is not an act, but a habit."[28] To gain a reputation for excellence necessitates delivering results whenever you're called upon. Hit-and-miss performers are neither trusted nor respected. On the other hand, those who repeatedly demonstrate competence gain credibility, and their credibility paves the way to influence.[29] That's the goal, isn't it? Our communities need more strong men who are in positions of leadership and working hard to make an impact. When we work faithfully, consistently, with excellence, we stand out and get noticed. Excellence fills the gap between average and exceptional. It's the ability to exceed expectations and consistently deliver superior quality.

---

27. https://twitter.com/bsnsports/status/918098886555787264
28. Will Durant, *The Story of Philosophy: The Lives and Opinions of the Greater Philosophers.* (New York: Simon & Schuster, 1926).
29. John Maxwell, *The 21 Irrefutable Laws of Leadership: Follow Them and People Will Follow You.* (Nashville, TN: Thomas Nelson, 1998).

In developing habits of excellence, leaders gain influence and stand out from the crowd for the right reasons.[30]

You don't have to be perfect. Your job doesn't need you to be perfect, and neither does your family. Acclaimed football coach of the hated Green Bay Packers (and I did say, hated!), Vince Lombardi, said, "Perfection is not attainable, but if we chase perfection we can catch excellence."[31] You just need to be committed to constantly improving, working to excel at everything you do. "To excel" literally means to go beyond average. Maxwell said that responsible people can be counted upon to do what is expected of them, but excellent people routinely do more than asked.

THE FIRST TIME'S A CHARM

Commit to taking pride in what you do whether you're at work where you receive a paycheck, at home where no one else will notice, or in your community where your efforts are voluntary. Be aware of how you look. Take pride in your appearance and the way others see you. Always present a sharp, crisp, and put together image. When you look sharp, you feel sharp. When you feel sharp, you will be sharp.

Develop the mindset of doing things right the first time so you can avoid having to do them over. Whenever you do something, ask the question, "If I don't do this right the first time, will I have time to do it over?" Truth be told, you probably won't have time to do it over. Even if you do, others will not want to wait for you to correct mistakes that could have

---

30. https://www.johnmaxwell.com/blog/excellence-a-sure-route-to-influence/
31. https://www.brainyquote.com/quotes/vince_lombardi_385070?src=t_excellence

been avoided in the first place. Time is money and money is time. And second-rate effort damages your reputation.

Not doing things right will end up costing you or someone else. The more time you take for rework, the less efficient you will be. Whether you work for yourself or for someone else, it's inevitable that rework will cost more money. When I worked in middle management for a Fortune 50 company, I learned people, especially employers, want to be as cost effective as possible. Being efficient and accurate the first time were principles that helped me achieve high success in sales, too. Right out of college, I entered the workforce on the ground floor. My knowledge and work ethic helped me show my value and earn a few quick promotions. I was thankful for my dad's lessons in hard work. They served me well then, and they serve me well now.

WHY IT MATTERS

I didn't have to be told that we were less fortunate than most of my school friends. I lived in the projects–subsidized government housing–until I was in junior high school. Once we were able to move out of there, we were only one step removed, and still remained on "that" side of town. We were still poor and didn't have a lot. When I was twelve years old, I started working in the corn fields for money to buy my own school clothes. My hard work also meant that I had a little spending money in my pocket.

We lived in Macomb, Illinois, a predominantly white town, where all the businesses were run by white people. I didn't know there was such a thing as a black-owned business. When I turned sixteen, my first real job was flipping burgers at McDonald's for $3.35 per hour. Macomb was a college town, so people gathered there from all over the state. Thankfully, I never personally experienced racism in trying to find employment. My dad lived a different experience. He had grown up in Macomb, too, and he knew there were some prejudiced people around town who had preconceived misconceptions about the character and work ethic of black people. He worked hard to prove himself and demonstrate that he was a good employee. He and his brothers worked hard to gain favor and a positive reputation in that town. When he taught me the principles of hard work, I understood that not only was I working to show myself to be a good worker, but since everyone around town knew that I was Mike's boy, I was working for his reputation as well.

In every walk of life, we earn a reputation. If we work hard and do well, we can earn a reputation of being a diligent employee. When given the opportunity, we should work to demonstrate that we will exceed expectations. This builds trust and affords us the opportunity to do business with that employer again. My dad's reputation helped open the doors for me. I work hard to help open doors for my kids. This is a lesson that not only applies to working, but to every part of life.

I have always had a desire to not disappoint people. This drives me to perform at a much higher level than is expected. For the most part, this trait is a good quality to have, but not always. In my quest for quality and excellence, I sometimes push myself, and those around me, too hard. This is especially true of my wife and family. Because I have such high expectations of myself, I tend to expect, and sometimes even demand, more of my family, too. Although, I think it's imperative to maintain the commitment to do things right the first time, I'm learning that I need to chill sometimes. (To my wife, boys, and Princess Katie: yes, I'm reading what I'm writing. I'll work on chilling out a little. However, remember, Daddy is still old school! So handle your business when you work, and I won't have to lay the smack down with another motivational talk.)

Chapter 5
Practice Teamwork

People are willing to do more for their team than they are willing to do for themselves.

I have always loved football. I grew up playing the game from the time I was a little tyke. Wait a minute, I don't believe I was ever little. I grew up playing football from the time I was a *"young"* tyke. I started playing when I was about eight or nine years old and didn't stop until I graduated college. As a kid, I would throw the ball around with my friends or anyone else who would catch it. The thing about football is that you can't play it by yourself, so I would often round up my friends to try to get a friendly neighborhood game going. We came to realize that three on three was about as few guys as we could have in order to have a fun game.

If we couldn't gather enough guys but were still itching to play, we would improvise and play the game called "500."

This is when one person would stand at one end of the field and throw or kick the ball into the air as high and far as he could. The remaining people would fight to catch the ball. If you caught it on the fly you would get 100 points, after one bounce you would get 75 points, after two bounces got you 50 points, and if you picked up the ball while it was still rolling you would get 25 points. The first person to accumulate 500 points won the game and would be the next to throw off. It wasn't the same as a good ole' game of playground tackle football, but sometimes it had to do. Looking back, I realize that 500 helped develop the fundamentals of the game, throwing and catching. We didn't know it at the time. We were just having fun and happy to be doing something related to football.

There was one time when a few of my friends and I happened to find a couple gallons of leftover paint. We had the bright idea to put it to use by painting our own makeshift football field on the grass at one of the open fields in the projects. We got weeks of fun out of that endeavor.

BABY FRIDGE

I was always big for my age. Even so, most people would say I was surprisingly quick and agile for my size. After the Chicago Bears drafted William "the Refrigerator" Perry in the first round of the 1985 draft, I adopted the nickname, Baby Fridge. The real Fridge was a beast, and everyone loved him. He was big, quick, and had a huge personality. Perry occasionally played fullback in goal line situations and set the then-record for the heaviest player to score a touchdown in the Super Bowl, at 335 pounds. I wasn't as big as the Fridge, but people were willing to move out of the way when I was running the ball. Furthermore, all of the guys around the way knew that when they picked me to be on their team, they were getting a versatile player who always played hard and would do anything to win.

As a result, when it came time to pick teams, I was usually chosen fairly early. That is right after Jerry and Terry Allen, the local neighborhood stud athletes. They were a couple years older than the rest of us so I didn't mind being picked after them, and Terry could juke anyone out of their shoes. They were both good, and if you were fortunate enough to have both of them on your team, you were most likely going to end up winning. The next pick was usually Carmen Hutcherson or Tony Carr. Then me. I could throw the ball pretty far, catch consistently, and run a little quicker than average. In playground pick up ball where you played without lineman, I was a solid early fourth-round pick in the neighborhood draft.

ORGANIZED FOOTBALL

When I was in junior high, I started playing organized football in the Macomb Football League. I had visions of playing quarterback and leading my team to the championship, however, since I nearly doubled the maximum weight limit for ball carriers, I was relegated to the blocking duty only. As you can imagine, I never got any smaller, so sadly, my days of touching the football were over. Thus, my career as lineman was born.

As an offensive and defensive lineman, I went on to play in high school and four years of college at Evangel University. I won many awards including entry into the College Football Hall of Fame, a true honor!

More importantly, I learned a lot about life by playing football and other organized sports. I had great coaches who taught me how to be a better football player on the field and a Christian man off the field. I am so thankful for coaches like Coach Moulden, Coach Barefield, and Coach Linn who not only coached me about the game, but also spoke into my life. I'll never forget these men and I wish to honor them every chance I get. They taught me much of what I know about teamwork. To work hard, never quit, be smart, and always give a maximum effort. They taught me to put the needs of the team above my own. They made it known that when the team wins, we all win. They helped me learn there is no "I" in team.

TEAM FIRST

In my junior year of college, I injured my knee playing intramural basketball during the off season. I went up for a rebound and, while in the air (most likely skying well above the rim), I was bumped causing me to land on my knee wrong. I landed on one leg and my knee hyper-extended. I heard a loud "pop" and knew something was wrong. I visited the team trainer. Her diagnosis was that there was no structural damage. She encouraged me to ice and rest it and watch for swelling, but thought I would be fine after a little rehab. The goal was to take it easy and do less stressful cardio in order to have me ready for the upcoming season, which was still months away.

I looked forward to my senior year and my team depended on me as a returning starter and one of the leaders of the offensive line. The previous year, I had won all-conference honors and I was picked as preseason All-American. Everyone expected me to have a good season and "make some noise," but this injury threatened all that.

All summer, whenever I worked out, I could tell something wasn't right with my knee. In retrospect, I should have gone to the doctor to get a professional opinion instead of only relying on the opinion of our team trainer. However, I waited until it was too late to explore treatment options like arthroscopic surgery. Had I had that surgery when it happened, even with a six-to-eight-week recovery, I would not have missed any of my senior year. Even so, when training camp started, I attempted to give it a go. It only took a few practices to realize my knee was not going to hold up.

About a week after training camp started, I went to the doctor and was told I could have surgery, but that meant I would miss most of the season. The alternative was that it was most likely a slight meniscus tear that I could play through, as long as I could handle the pain. After talking with my teammates and coaches they told me they needed me and didn't want me out for most of the season. I opted to "play through the pain." And pain it was! Before each game, I would wrap my knee, put on my brace, and pop as many ibuprofens as was safe and legal. I played the best I could on that bum knee because the team needed me.

Everyone knew I wasn't one hundred percent and that I had limited mobility. Every now and then I would tweak my knee and have to miss a couple of plays, but I pushed through and played the whole year. After each game, I would go back to my room, or to Angie's apartment and lay on the couch. I would hurt for days after each game, the whole season. So why did I do it? Because my team said they needed me, and I was willing to do more for the team then I would do for myself.

THERE'S SOMETHING SPECIAL ABOUT BEING ON A TEAM

There's nothing like being on a good team. Whether it's a winning sports team, a strong work team, a unified ministry team, or a loving home team – when you have the privilege of being a part of a good team, it will help you flourish and grow. Teams help you develop skills, character, and influence. Your team will help you stay balanced in your life and develop emotionally, spiritually, physically, intellectually, and socially. Being a part of a team helps you stay on the journey through being accountable to other people and not just yourself. On a good team, each member has each other's back and offers help, encouragement, and honest feedback.

Patrick Lencioni talks about how members of truly cohesive teams behave. Three things that stand out to me from his list. He says cohesive teams trust one another, hold one another accountable, and focus on achievement of collective results.[32]

A great way to help your team come together is to strive for the 5 C's of teamwork. I've seen different people list

---

32. Patrick Lencioni, *The Five Dysfunctions of a Team: A Leadership Fable*. (San Francisco: Jossey Bass, 2002).

five different characteristics, but since this is my book, I'm going to say the 5 C's stand for communication, camaraderie, commitment, confidence, and coachability.[33] When you begin working on each of these areas, you will notice significant changes to your teammates and yourself.

- Communication must be open and clear. All team members must be free to express themselves without fear or judgment.
- Camaraderie is having mutual trust and friendship among members of the team as they spend time together.
- Commitment is an agreement or pledge between team members to work together and support one another.
- Confidence is the feeling or belief that team members can rely on and trust each other.
- Coachability is an individual's willingness and ability to seek, be receptive to, and act on constructive feedback to drive individual development and improve performance.[34]

ASSEMBLING YOUR TEAM

Get your team together. Life is hard and you are not going to be able to be strong and Man UP like God intends for you to be without the help of people around you. The example we see in Scripture is of Paul having Barnabas pouring into his life, mentoring, and teaching him. Then in return, Paul has Timothy that he is mentoring and teaching the ways of the faith. This is the perfect example for each of us, we should always have someone pouring into us, while at the same time, we should be pouring into someone else.

---

33. Google search for 5 C's of a Team.
34. https://coachabilityconsultants.com/what-is-coachability/

It's not a one-way flow. If you only have people pouring into you, helping you, and teaching you, it will be easy for you to grow arrogant and unapproachable. At the same time, if you are always pouring out to others, spending most of your time helping, and mentoring others, you may wear yourself out and get burned out. This isn't good for anyone.

While I was the pastor of an inner-city church in St. Louis, our congregation consisted of a few hundred people who were mostly poor and needy. They often needed food, clothes, coats, school supplies, etc. I challenged them to get to the point where they weren't always receiving stuff. We put programs and educational opportunities in place so they could grow and improve their lives. I challenged them to not only eat, but to eventually help us feed others. Otherwise, they were prone to stay in the condition they were in and would not advance to the point where they could produce the fruit that God intended for them. We provided the support they needed to improve their lives and eventually become productive members of society. That's the value of a team.

LEARN TO BE A GOOD TEAM PLAYER

It's not just about looking for good teammates around you, but it's also about becoming a good team player. John Maxwell has a book that will help you develop the essential qualities necessary to be a good team player. In addition to the 5 C's, he says we need to develop other qualities like being dependable and disciplined. He writes about being adaptable and willing to change for the sake of the team. He encourages us to always be improving ourselves which in return will help improve the team. As well, he spends time talking about being selfless team members, and being willing to sacrifice for the good of the team.[35]

The 1980's San Francisco 49ers are one of the most memorable examples of a team working together and sacrificing for the good of the team. The Niners were by far the greatest team of that decade after winning four Super Bowls. That team was full of Hall of Famers: Joe Montana, Jerry Rice, Ronnie Lott, Steve Young, Charles Haley, Fred Dean, and coached by Bill Walsh and George Seifert. They were exciting to watch because they exemplified commitment to each other in a way that other teams didn't.

Safety Ronnie Lott famously had part of his pinky amputated so that he wouldn't miss a game during the 1985-86 season. It was the last game of the season, and the 49ers were playing against the Dallas Cowboys. While trying to make a tackle on running back Timmy Newsome, Ronnie Lott shattered his pinkie finger. The playoffs were just around the corner, and Ronnie Lott had a big decision to make that would change the rest of his life. Team doctors put a seemingly insane choice to Lott. He could either: 1) Put a pin in his finger and it would heal in two months, but he'd miss the rest of the season, or 2) Amputate the pinkie finger from the first joint up and play right away. Ronnie Lott chose amputation. A chunk of his pinkie finger was chopped off. There is no way this would even be a consideration today, but this is exactly what happened.[36] That's a crazy example of a person being willing to do more for the team than they are willing to do for themselves. That man has gone through the rest of his

---
35. John C. Maxwell, *The 17 Essential Qualities of a Team Player: Becoming the Kind of Person Every Team Wants* (Nashville, TN: Thomas Nelson, 2002).
36. https://www.sports-king.com/ronnie-lott-amputated-finger-3327/

life with a piece of his pinky missing, so he could play and help his team win a Super Bowl. Football players are crazy sometimes.

I've seen other examples of this in my lifetime. Brett Favre led his team on the field the day after his father died. Dwayne Wade put off shoulder surgery and chose to play through pain in order to help his team try and win a championship. Finally, like him or not, you have to give it up for Terrell Owens. Famously known as "TO". He needed ankle surgery, and his surgeon was hesitant to clear him to play in Super Bowl 39 against the Patriots. The medical world thought he was crazy when he ran onto the field. Owens surprised everyone by playing 62 of 72 offensive snaps and catching nine passes for 122 yards in that game. It might have been the most courageous performance in Super Bowl history.[37]

What makes these men do these things? They understand the significance of teamwork. Let us follow their lead and Man UP. Be strong and be a man who is willing to do more for the team than you are willing to do for yourself.

---

37. https://www.sports-king.com/ronnie-lott-amputated-finger-3327/.

Section 2:
Be Observant
Learn the Lord's Commands

- **Chapter 6** First Things First
- **Chapter 7** Daily Grind
- **Chapter 8** Discipline
- **Chapter 9** Sacrifice

Chapter 6
First Things First

Before he relinquished the throne, King David wanted his son to understand that being committed to putting God first in all he did as the king and leader of Israel, was the key to his success. David had great success during his forty year reign and people sang songs about his greatness. Even though he made many mistakes during his lifetime, God blessed him and considered him to be a man after His own heart.[38] David trusted God and sought to glorify Him and put Him first all of his life.

When David was a young shepherd boy tending his father's sheep something was special about him. I imagined this is where God began to see his heart and true character. He was a strong, faithful, and courageous young man who killed a lion and a bear who tried to attack the flock (see 1 Samuel 17:36). This was a display of God's miraculous

---
38. 1 Samuel 13:14, NIV.

hand being with David before he was even called to be a great leader. Then after being anointed to be the next king of Israel to replace Saul, David stayed humble and true to who he was. When given the opportunity to represent the God of heaven and the nation of Israel in battle against Goliath, David didn't flinch because he knew that the same God who delivered him from the paw of the lion and the paw of the bear would deliver him from the hand of Goliath (1 Samuel 17:37). David trusted God and put Him first.

When David was on the run from a jealous King Saul who tried to kill him on numerous occasions, David trusted God to protect him and vindicate him. He rejected the urging to take matters into his own hands and acquire the kingdom by blood. On two different occasions he had the opportunity to kill Saul and he refused to do so, saying that he would not raise his hand against the Lord's anointed.[39] He was willing to trust God by patiently waiting for things to unfold in His timing (1 Samuel 24 and 26).

Upon hearing of Saul's death, realizing that it was time to ascend to the throne, David inquired of God to see what he should do (2 Samuel 2:1). I know if it were me, after having to wait for a few decades, I would have walked into the palace like I was the man! Wassup?! David was determined to honor God in everything and make sure God's will was done above all else.

Once he was king, David continued to put God first when he brought the ark of God to Jerusalem, the Jewish kingdom's capital city (see 2 Samuel 6). The Ark of the Covenant was one of Israel's symbols of faith and God's presence. The

---

39. 1 Samuel 26:9–11, NIV.

contents of which included the tables of the Mosaic law, a pot of manna, and the rod of Aaron.[40] David made this one of his first acts after becoming king. He wanted God's presence near him at all times.

All throughout the Old Testament, we see a pattern of King David putting God first in all that he does. Even after David committed adultery with Bathsheba, conspired to murder her husband, and then covered it up, he didn't turn from God. When confronted with his sin by the prophet Nathan, he quickly repented, restoring God to the throne of his heart (see 2 Samuel 12). This was much different than how King Saul responded after he sinned. He wanted to downplay his sin and represent to the people like everything was good (see 1 Samuel 15).

Time and time again, David demonstrated that strong men know what God requires of them, seek to put Him first in their lives, and are committed to spending as much time as possible in God's presence.

PRAYING GRANDMA

Can I encourage you to Man UP and be committed to putting God first in your life? There is a reason why grandmothers all over the world have always been known as strong pillars of faith. Their wisdom from observing all that happens in life has led them to the conclusion that Solomon also came to with near the end of his life. Ecclesiastes 12:13–14, NIV, is worth mentioning, "Now all has been heard; here is the conclusion of the matter: Fear God and keep his commandments, for this

---
40. Chad Napier. "What Was the Ark of the Covenant? Its Meaning and Significance." https://www.christianity.com/wiki/bible/what-was-the-ark-of-the-covenant-its-meaning-and-significance.html.

is the duty of all mankind. For God will bring every deed into judgment, including every hidden thing, whether it is good or evil." He came to observe that in the end, it's all about God. So, Solomon encouraged all of us to fear God and keep His commands.

If you asked most people if they believed in heaven, they would say yes. Nearly two-thirds of Americans, in a national survey, said they believe they will go to heaven. Only one half of one percent said they were hell-bound, according to the poll by Oxnard, California, Barna Research Group,[41] an independent marketing research firm which has tracked trends related to beliefs, values, and behaviors since 1984. The same survey found that seventy-six percent of Americans believe there is a heaven while only seventy-one percent believe there is a hell. These numbers are the same as a decade ago.

This article also said that two out of three people think they are on their way to heaven. This belief is contrary to what the Bible teaches us. Matthew 7:14, NIV, says, "Small is the gate and narrow the road that leads to life, and only a few find it." People are being deceived into thinking they are going to heaven, but they have a false sense of assurance of this. They think they only have to be a good person and they will make it. They really don't know the truth. Some don't read the Bible enough to know what it teaches and many others have rejected the Bible as the ultimate source of truth.

---

41. *Tampa Bay Times*, "Survey Finds Few Volunteers for Hell," https://www.tampabay.com/archive/2003/11/02/survey-finds-few-volunteers-for-hell/?outputType=amp.

MORAL RELATIVISM

Too many people believe there are no absolute truths anymore. They live like what is morally right or wrong varies from person to person or from society to society. This is a false worldview that is misleading a lot of people and confusing the younger generation. People don't appear to be seekers of truth today; instead they are known for speaking their truth. People are calling right wrong, and wrong right. The truth is being attacked and challenged in every way.

Author and pastor, Erwin Lutzer, speaks about this in his book, *No Reason to Hide*. He said that at one time in America people generally believed that "the truth" was a reality outside ourselves, and we could dialogue back and forth, agreeing or disagreeing with one another, as to what the truth was. Those days are gone. In our woke culture, there is no "truth out there" because truth is now "in me" and it's whatever we each say it is. With no compelling search for truth, all that is left is the quest for power. Reasonable dialogue has given way to entrenched, self-congratulatory selfism. And no ground can be conceded to those who disagree with "my standpoint."[42] One of the reasons I wanted to write this book was to motivate men to discover God's Truth and encourage them to stand on it. Manning UP requires you to know truth, and stand on it.

Christ Jesus said, "Ye shall know the truth, and the truth shall make you free" (John 8:32, KJV). Moral relativism conveys the belief that what's right for me is right for me and what's right for you is right for you. This is what society

---
42. Erwin W. Lutzer. *No Reason to Hide: Standing for Christ in a Collapsing Culture* (Eugene, OR: Harvest House Publishers, 2022).

is offering us today, but it's breeding mass deception. When adopted by individuals or a society, moral relativism will lead to serious consequences. We are losing our sense of being able to distinguish between right and wrong. We have people justifying their sin, unashamed of their sin, proud of their sin, and therefore, unrepentant of their sin.

THE TRUTH ABOUT MORAL RELATIVISM

The truth is there is only one way to heaven and it comes through believing in Jesus Christ, God's only Son (see John 14:6). You have to believe that He died to pay the price for your sin. Then accept the forgiveness that comes from His blood washing away your sin. His sacrifice makes it possible for you to be a new creation and receive eternal life. By asking Jesus for forgiveness and accepting Him into your heart, you will be saved. It is only then that you will reap the reward of eternal life in heaven with Him.

It's all about loving God. However, most people don't really know what this truly means. Thoroughly reading of Scripture leads us to conclude that loving God means that we are obedient to His commands. Let me break it down as simply as I can by offering straightforward verses:

- **1 John 5:3, NIV:** *"This is love for God: to keep His commands . . ."*
- **John 14:15, NIV:** *"If you love me, keep my commands"*
- **John 14:21, NIV:** *"Whoever has my commands and keeps them is the one who loves me."*

- **John 14:23, NIV:** *"Jesus replied, 'Anyone who loves me will obey my teaching.'"*
- **John 14:24, NIV:** *"Anyone who does not love me will not obey my teaching."*

Seems pretty clear, doesn't it? You have to show God you love Him by doing what His Word tells you to do. Too many people have a wrong understanding of what it means to love God–and it shows. Since they are not walking in obedience to Him and to what He requires of us according to Scripture, they are not experiencing the blessings that come from obedience. They are frustrated and don't understand why their life is tougher than it needs to be. Not to mention, this false understanding of loving God may cost them dearly when they stand before Him and He says, "Depart from me, I never knew you."[43]

Heaven is the ultimate reward we are living for. The reward is only given to those with the right answer. Too many people falsely believe they are getting this reward, yet they are not even close to the right answer. We, as Christians, should be looking for opportunities to show people the truth. Witnessing is something that a lot of people believe should be left up to young people at their high schools. The Bible gives a charge to all believers to fulfill the Great Commission to go into all nations and make disciples. We must share with the world that Jesus is the answer and the only way to make it to heaven.

PURPOSE DRIVEN LIFE

In his book, *Purpose Driven Life*, Rick Warren teaches that we are placed on earth for two reasons. The first is to have

---
43. Matthew 7:21–32, NIV.

a relationship with God, and the second is to help as many people as possible have that same relationship.[44] Once we know that we are good with Jesus, then we must get busy helping others get right with God. This may mean you have to introduce them to Jesus by leading them to Him. However, that's not where our assignment ends. When Jesus gave us the Great Commission, He sent us out to go and make disciples of all nations, not just converts.[45] Discipleship calls for us to remain in their life and help them learn to observe the Lord's commands and be obedient to them. Specifically, Jesus told us to make sure people get baptized. Then we are to teach them to obey everything He has commanded us. That's a lot for all of us to learn.

ROMANS ROAD

We have to start somewhere. Now that you know your bigger purpose, let me teach you the most simple way to start. There is a way of leading someone to the Lord that every Christian needs to know, it's called the Romans Road. It's four Scriptures out of the Book of Romans that you should memorize and use often in witnessing.

> 1. **Romans 3:23:** *"For all have sinned and fall short of the glory of God."*
> 2. **Romans 6:23:** *"For the wages of sin is death, but the gift of God is eternal life in Christ Jesus our Lord."*
> 3. **Romans 5:8:** *"But God demonstrates his own love

---
44. Rick Warren. *The Purpose-Driven Life: What on Earth Am I Here For?* (Grand Rapids, MI: Zondervan, 2002).
45. Matthew 28:19–20, NIV.

for us in this: While we were still sinners, Christ died for us."

4. **Romans 10:9–10:** *"That if you confess with your mouth, 'Jesus is Lord,' and believe in your heart that God raised him from the dead, you will be saved. For it is with your heart that you believe and are justified, and it is with your mouth that you confess and are saved."*

There is only one requirement for each individual to obtain this eternal life and live in eternity with God. That requirement is the belief in and acceptance of the sacrifice of His Son for our salvation.

The Bible says it several times: the only way to make it to heaven is through Jesus Christ. The world needs to know this even though it's a tough pill for many to swallow. Don't be deceived, there is a heaven and there is a hell. Everyone who has ever been born will spend eternity in one of these places. The Bible teaches us that these facts are absolutes and are indeed true. God doesn't want us to perish and has provided a way for us to receive eternal life, but we have to accept it. Check out this well-known Scripture in a different translation:

"For God so [greatly] loved and dearly prized the world, that He [even] gave His [One and] only begotten Son, so that whoever believes and trusts in Him [as Savior] shall not perish, but have eternal life" (John 3:16, Amplified Bible).

If you are reading this book, I hope you already know this truth. However, knowing it is not enough. You have to believe this enough to take action. Once you have taken action yourself and asked for forgiveness for your sins, you need to share this truth with other people. That's our purpose in this life. To know God and to make Him known.

I believe that God brings other people into our lives so that we can share the gospel with them. Do you realize that there are people who will only hear the gospel if you share it with them? That's going to require for you to be a strong man who knows God's commands and then has the courage to live them out loud. We have to Man UP and tell people the truth.

TAKING IT TO THE STREETS

I remember the first time I went out street witnessing. I was in high school and our youth pastor took us to the University of Illinois and told us to go out and tell someone about Jesus. I was so scared. I mean, I was only in high school and most of the people around me were in college. They didn't want some pimpled-face high school student stopping them and trying to push Jesus on them. At least that's what I thought.

At this point, I imagine you are waiting for my testimony of how I overcame my fear and shared the gospel and went around leading dozens of people to Jesus that day. Well, don't hold your breath! I wimped out that day–big time! I approached a few people but I wasn't brave enough to even start the conversation about Jesus. I left there feeling like a failure. Can you identify?

Years later, I have seen how that experience eventually gave me the courage to approach strangers and strike up a conversation with them. Sometimes, these conversations have led to me planting a seed about Jesus and other times, they ended in me praying with people to receive Christ, right then and there. I Manned UP! Now, I teach other people how to street evangelize. I believe that when we know God's Word, we understand that He desires for us to share His gospel with anyone, anywhere, at any time. This is Manning UP!

Chapter 7
Daily Grind

Throughout our marriage, my wife has always had the goal of having our family eat dinner together at the table a couple times a week. That's the goal; however, with five kids who were very active in school activities and sports, we didn't always realize that goal. I vividly remember one of these occasions a few years ago. When they were younger, it was always a struggle to get our boys to eat anything other than bland and simple food like chicken nuggets or frozen pizza. It's interesting to note that we have never had this problem with Katie. That girl will try anything and eat anything. Ang thinks it's because she used to feed her different spices when she was a baby. She swears that this expanded Katie's palate and made her a less picky eater.

Anyway, we were never surprised when one of the boys would refuse to eat what was in front of them. I wouldn't be exaggerating to say we heard the, "I don't' like it, I don't like it" chant two to three nights a week. It was maddening. So, on this one particular night I wasn't surprised that it was happening again. However, I wasn't in the mood for it that night. Sometimes the daily grind wears me down and I just want to come home and eat a nice peaceful dinner. You know what I mean?

It is surprising to me that any of *my boys* would have a problem eating what's placed in front of them. I mean, judging by the size of their father, you wouldn't think they would have a problem eating anything. I am a big guy of 300-plus pounds. My size served me well when I played offensive line in college. Like most young dads, I always wanted my boys to play football and represent the family in the NFL. With four boys, I thought for sure one of them would grow to be six-foot-five-inches tall and 250 pounds, and end up being a linebacker for the Chicago Bears. A brotha can dream, can't he?

Back to the story. I always had the rule that I would not ask my kids to eat anything that I wasn't willing to eat. I adopted this rule one time after tasting baby food out of a jar–that stuff is atrocious! The food we placed in front of them was always good food and nothing that stretched the taste buds too far. Angie is an excellent cook and takes joy in feeding her kids–all of us. Hence, it always baffled me when the boys didn't want to eat. Sometimes they refused to even try the food before starting the chant. This would infuriate both my wife and me. It still does. We have always had the rule that our kids had to try everything at least one time. If they at least tried it and decided they didn't like it, we would then negotiate a portion that would have to be consumed. But they had to for sure try it.

On this particular night, my oldest son Trey started the "I don't like it, I don't like it" chant as soon as the food touched the table. Immediately Michael joined in indicating he didn't like it either, before either of them even took a bite of anything, mind you. By the sight of the food alone they declared they didn't like it and were not planning to partake of the delicacies of that evening. Well, they didn't use such flowery words, but you get the point! That night, I hunkered down and realized I was in for a long evening. After the day I had had, I wasn't about to back down to little jabronies who didn't want to eat the food that my wife prepared.

I started giving them the lecture—you know, all the usual stuff. "Trey, eat your food. You don't know if you don't like it until you try it. There are hungry kids all over the world who would love to trade places with you tonight."

Nothing was working. These kids were sitting there like stone-faced statues, not budging a bit. I realized that I wasn't getting anywhere with Trey, so I turned to Michael. "Come on buddy, eat your food. Your mother spent a lot of time slaving over the stove so that you can enjoy this meal."

Full disclosure: she didn't really slave over the stove. Ang is more of a Crock-Pot and microwave girl. I imagine she spent a lot of time waiting for the microwave timer to go off. But that's besides the point, and he didn't need to know how it was prepared. I kept going. "Fellas, you know the deal, you have to at least try your food. Daddy's running out of patience. Let's go! You never know if you like it if you don't try it."

THE STRUGGLE IS REAL

Nothing was working and those little boys were committed to standing their ground that night. I remember growing so angry, so quickly–and I was ready to lay the smack down on these little boys over something so small. Sometimes anger comes out of nowhere. People can push our buttons and get us upset, pushing us to do something that we may regret. Have you ever had an experience like that?

I didn't want to have to deal with my kids at that time. I was tired after a long day of work and was ready to eat a good meal and kick back and relax. Yet, it was clear that I had a problem I had to deal with. I've come to realize that the problems we face, no matter how big or small, will either defeat us or develop us, depending on how we respond to them. Unfortunately, most people fail to see how God wants to use problems for good in their lives. They react foolishly and resent their problems rather than pausing to consider what benefit they might bring.

DEALING WITH PROBLEMS

As the king of Israel, David had to deal with problems all the time. One in particular was a continual problem he had with the leader of his army, Joab. In establishing his kingdom, David needed fighting men around him to fight the necessary wars to establish Israel as a sovereign nation.

Joab was David's nephew and was most likely with David while he was in exile on the run from King Saul. In 1 Samuel

22:1 we are told that soon after David fled from Saul, his brothers and father's household joined him in exile, along with about 400 other men. Saul likely would have been eager to kill not just David, but his family as well. So, while not mentioned by name, Joab likely joined up with David along with the rest of David's family at this time, early in his exile.[46]

When David became king, he chose Jerusalem to be the capital of the united kingdom, but the problem was that Jerusalem was occupied by the Jebusites. Joab led a successful attack on Jerusalem and, as a result, was made commander-in-chief of David's army. Throughout the years, David made alliances with other tribes and kingdoms and sometimes this called for him to make military changes. At each turn, Joab was there undermining David's decisions and imposing his own will. Joab killed Abner and Amasa,[47] both innocent men that David had installed as leaders of Israel in place of Joab. He killed them in cold blood to retain his power and might within the military of Israel. David knew that Joab was a headache, but sadly, he never really dealt with him.

At the end of his reign, David passed the Joab problem down to his son Solomon. He reminded Solomon of how evil and wicked Joab had been all throughout his reign and advised him to deal with Joab according to his wisdom.[48] Growing up in the palace, Solomon had witnessed Joab's wickedness firsthand. When he became king, Solomon's brother Adonijah attempted an insurrection; Joab made the deadly mistake of

---

46. Ed Jarrett, "Joab, a Ruthless, But Fiercely Loyal Commander," modified September 16, 2021, https://www.biblestudytools.com/bible-study/topical-studies/joab-a-ruthless-but-fiercely-loyal-commander.html
47. 1 Kings 2:5, NIV.
48. 1 Kings 2:6, NIV.

siding with Adonijah. Given Joab's ambition to rule the army, I think it likely that Adonijah had offered that position to him. So, he made a fateful choice that, in the end, cost him his life. Solomon quickly had Joab put to death.[49]

Through David and Solomon handling Joab, we learn a valuable lesson about how God uses the problems in our lives. God is at work in your life–even when you do not recognize it or understand it. But it's much easier and profitable when you cooperate with Him. A while ago, I heard a sermon about how–if we allow Him to–God will use the problems in each of our lives to:

> *1.* **God uses problems to DIRECT you.** *Sometimes God must light a fire under you to get you moving. Problems often point us in a new direction and motivate us to change*
> 2. **God uses problems to INSPECT you.** *People are like tea bags . . . if you want to know what's inside them, just drop them into hot water! Has God tested your faith with a problem?*
> *3.* **God uses problems to CORRECT you.** *Some lessons we learn only through pain and failure. It's likely that as a child your parents told you not to touch a hot stove. But you probably learned by being burned. Sometimes we only learn the value of something . . . health, money, a relationship . . . by losing it.*
> *4.* **God uses problems to PROTECT you.** *A problem can be a blessing in disguise if it prevents*

---

49. 1 Kings 2:34, NIV.

you from being harmed by something more serious.
5. God uses problems to PERFECT you. *Problems, when responded to correctly, are character builders. God is far more interested in your character than your comfort. Your relationship to God and your character are the only two things you're going to take with you into eternity.*[50]

OBSERVE AND LEARN

By watching all that his father went through, Solomon learned from David's life experience and went on to be known as the wisest man to have ever lived. Throughout his lifetime, he observed his father, who made it a habit of learning the Lord's commands. In Psalms 119, which is ironically the longest chapter in the Bible, David starts by saying; "Blessed are those whose lives have integrity, *those who follow the teachings of the Lord. Blessed are those who obey his written instructions. They wholeheartedly search for him."*[51]

The Bible speaks a lot about knowledge and wisdom, specifically in the Book of Proverbs, which was primarily written by King Solomon. For years, I have begun each day by reading at least one chapter in Proverbs. I would encourage you to implement this practice into your life. There are thirty-one chapters in the Book of Proverbs and thirty-one days in most months. Whatever day of the month it is, read that corresponding chapter of Proverbs. I challenge you to do "The Proverbs Challenge" every month for a year and see how much wisdom you will gain from this easy daily habit.

50. *Mighty Arrows magazine.* https://www.suscopts.org/mightyarrows/vol4_no1/fiveways.pdf
51. Psalms 119:1–2, NIV.

The purpose and theme of the Book of Proverbs is summed up in the first few verses of the first chapter. Check Proverbs 1:2–7 in the New Century Version:

> They teach wisdom and self-control;
> they will help you understand wise words.
> They will teach you how to be wise and self-controlled
> and will teach you to do what is honest and fair and right.
> They make the uneducated smarter
> and give knowledge and sense to the young.
> Wise people can also listen and learn;
> even smart people can find good advice in these words.
> Then anyone can understand wise words and stories,
> the words of the wise and their riddles.
> Knowledge begins with respect for the Lord,
> but fools hate wisdom and self-control.

There are so many truths in the Book of Proverbs that will teach you to make better choices and live a healthier life. People are always looking for advice about how to live a better, more prosperous life. They turn to fortune cookies, horoscopes, psychic friends, counselors and therapists–you name it. Although they may not admit it, people want to be told what to do in order to improve their life.

Can I encourage you to look no further than the Bible? It's the ultimate source of truth, wisdom, and knowledge. God knows what you are going through in your daily grind, and He knows what you need. His wisdom is irrefutable and timeless. His knowledge is limitless and infinite.

WISDOM IS ALL AROUND US

Back to the dinner battles. While Trey was chanting, "I don't like it, I don't like it," Michael, who was only two or three years old at the time, was hit with a bit of wisdom. He stopped his protest and joined me by rationally telling Trey, "We better eat our food or else you know we are going to get a spanking." At least that's what I think he said. I'm not sure because it seemed way too simple for a two year old to logically make this deduction.

Now trust me, I've always been open to accept all the parenting help I can get, but there were a few reasons I wasn't open to Michael joining in. First of all, who was he to tell Trey to eat his food when just the night before he had gotten in trouble for refusing to eat? Secondly, I knew his comments would only add fuel to the fire. Trey wouldn't look too kindly at his brother affirming what Dad was saying about eating. They were brothers and supposed to have each other's back, especially against their parents. In Trey's eyes, Michael should have been loyal and completely on his side. The final reason I wasn't open to his input is because I was way too prideful to have a two-year-old helping me parent! Talk about a blow to my pride.

I immediately told Michael to be quiet and that I didn't need his help. With his deep, raspy voice, he looked me dead in the eye and said, "Sorry, I talk too much, don't I?" It took everything I had inside me to hold back the laughter and focus on the task at hand. These boys were going to eat this food that night if it killed me. They had to learn this lesson once and for all. As all this is happening, while I was locked in this epic battle, out of the corner of my eye, I noticed Ang was about to choke on her food because she was laughing so hard. Kids say the darndest things, don't they?

I remember thinking that Michael reminded me of some people that I had dealt with in ministry that day. It's hard for some people to be told what to do, and many don't want to be corrected when the focus is on them. Yet, they are ready to jump in and tell someone else what they need to do or how to live. Ironically, the Bible speaks about hypocritical behavior. First take the log out of your own eye before you try to take the speck out of your neighbor's eye.[52]

Michael was only two, maybe three years old, so I couldn't expect him to know any better. He was a little too young to comprehend these things, but you aren't, my friend. There are lessons in life that we, as adults, should know but don't always know. We often lack fundamental knowledge and wisdom. Too many people say pretty much everything that's on their mind–a lot of it inappropriate and ill-timed–without thinking. Their lack of wisdom shows their ignorance and reveals their social ineptness. By being observant to the Word of God, they would gain the wisdom and discretion necessary to have healthy conversations with people. In this day and age, we need more men who use God's wisdom to lead them in all of their interactions.

MEN OF ISSACHAR

I was recently reminded of the two hundred men of the tribe of Issachar.[53] Men of Issachar were men of alignment,

---

52. Matthew 7:5, New Revised Standard Version.
53. 1 Chronicles 12:32, NIV.

aligned with the prophetic voice in the land and engaged in God's strategies of the time. They served as advisors to King David. They discerned God's truth and spoke up. They advised rulers on what was good, what was true, and what was right. I believe we can be like those advisors of Issachar. We have been entrusted with the truth, not to shrink from it, but to stand with the clarity and conviction missing in our day. We are to understand our times and what our nation should do. We are to speak what is true, and we can learn this by gleaming of all the wisdom available to us in God's Word.

A FEW OF MY FAVORITE PROVERBS

Here are a few of my favorite proverbs. Many of these are maxims that you have possibly heard before but maybe didn't realize they came from the Bible:

- *Trust in the Lord with all your heart and lean not on your own understanding; in all your ways acknowledge him, and he will make your paths straight (Proverbs 3:5–6, NIV).*
- *Wisdom is the most important thing; so get wisdom. If it costs everything you have, get understanding (Proverbs 4:7, NCV).*
- *The man of integrity walks securely, but he who takes crooked paths will be found out. (Proverbs 10:9, NIV).*
- *Hatred stirs up trouble, but love forgives all wrongs. (Proverbs 10:12, NCV).*
- *If you talk a lot, you are sure to sin; if you are wise, you will keep quiet (Proverbs 10:19, NCV).*
- *Fools will believe anything, but the wise think about what they do (Proverbs 14:15, NCV).*

- *Those who work hard make a profit, but those who only talk will be poor (Proverbs 14:23, NCV).*
- *A gentle answer turns away wrath, but a harsh word stirs up anger (Proverbs 15:1, NIV).*
- *Commit to the Lord whatever you do, and your plans will succeed (Proverbs 16:3, NIV).*
- *Anyone who answers without listening is foolish and confused (Proverbs 18:13, NCV).*
- *The tongue has the power of life and death (Proverbs 18:21, NIV).*
- *Listen to advice and accept instruction, and in the end you will be wise (Proverbs 19:20, NIV).*
- *Those who are careful about what they say keep themselves out of trouble (Proverbs 21:23, NCV).*
- *If you give up when trouble comes, it shows that you are weak (Proverbs 24:10, NCV).*
- *As iron sharpens iron, so people can improve each other (Proverbs 27:17, NCV).*
- *As water reflects a face, so a man's heart reflects the man (Proverbs 27:19, NIV).*

I could go on and on listing my favorite proverbs. I would love to take the time and explain what each of the aforementioned Scriptures means to me, but I won't. I will let them stand alone and allow the Holy Spirit to use them to speak personally to your heart. I encourage you not to move past these proverbs too quickly. Take some time to stop and meditate on what each of them means. Think about how these truths can apply to your life and help you live a more godly life. In the Bible, Jesus often says that those who have ears to hear, should hear! He is calling for people to pay careful attention. It's another way of saying, "Listen up! Pay close attention!" That's what I would say to you when reading these proverbs. Make sure you are extremely observant in learning God's commands and then be diligent about putting into practice what you have learned. That's Manning UP!

Chapter 8
Discipline

I learned this from playing football.

Merriam-Webster's Dictionary has a couple of definitions for the word *discipline*. There's one that I think works best for this chapter:

Discipline:
- *Punishment intended to correct or train.*
- *Training that is expected to produce a specific character or pattern of behavior, especially training that produces moral or mental improvement.*

These definitions are what comes to mind when I think of the word *discipline*. Training and punishment both help develop certain skills or behavior which lead to establishing effective boundaries. Discipline helps us set up parameters in life by which we should recognize and respect. We should try to live our lives within these boundaries and do our best to not go outside of them.

For me, learning discipline has been a process. There have been times in my life when the fruit of living a disciplined life has been more evident than at other times. As I reflect on my life, three specific times stand out as memorable occasions for me to learn more about discipline and all that surrounds it.

1. AS A CHILD, MY MOM ENDEAVORED TO TEACH ME DISCIPLINE

I was always a strong-willed young man. Way back when, people said I was extremely hardheaded and stubborn. I'd like to point out that I have never been as stubborn as someone that I may be married to... but I'm not going to mention any names. Let's just say, I liked to have my way. My real dad wasn't around, but my mom was. And she didn't play! She was tough, strong, and stern. She worked hard to keep me on the right path. I didn't like it at the time, but now I am thankful for her diligence.

She taught me the valuable lesson that it's the parents' responsibility to teach their kids discipline at an early age. She believed that parents should establish boundaries for their children, and when those kids went outside of the boundaries, they should be punished. She was extremely old school too, which meant that she would regularly go upside my head.

When a child is young, in the toddler stage, often the punishment for crossing the boundaries is physical discipline, a spanking. Today, there is much debate about whether spanking is a good or bad thing. I don't remember my mom contemplating that at all. I've come to conclude that although

I agree it is acceptable and appropriate to spank children, it's not the only form of discipline that should be used. The Bible teaches it is acceptable and even prudent to spank your children at times, and for me, the Bible is the ultimate source of truth and wisdom.

SPARE THE ROD, SPOIL THE CHILD

Proverbs 13:24 says that he who spares the rod hates his son, but he who loves him is careful to discipline him. The Bible could not be any clearer on the acceptable nature of spanking a child. I know personally, spankings and the fear of a spanking stopped me from doing several bad things when I was young. Have you ever been spanked by a big black mom? I have! When done in the right way, spanking a child leaves a reminder to them that what they did was wrong. It was so wrong that they received a physical reminder of this that left a lasting reminder of a sore backside. If they don't want their bottom to feel like this again, in the future they should refrain from repeating the act that caused their bottom to feel this way. It shows the kids that their parents love them enough to help them improve and mature.

Proverbs 19:18, NIV, says, "Discipline your children, for in that there is hope; do not be a willing party to their death." This passage calls for swift and immediate discipline. Parents, discipline your kids while there is still hope. Don't get caught up in thinking there will be a more appropriate time or that maybe the problem will correct itself. Don't take the chance of waiting and allow the bad attitude or wrong action to turn into a bigger problem. Discipline them immediately while there is still a good chance that they will listen and correct the behavior. As soon as you recognize that there appears to be a corrupt disposition in them, check it immediately! Do it before the bad attitude takes root and turns into a bad habit. Discipline your son while there is still hope, before it's too late. It's much easier to pluck up weeds as soon as they spring up. The same is true with disciplining our children.

My mom believed this to be true. Back in the day (for those unfamiliar with the term "back in the day," that means when I was younger), I never heard my mom say anything like, "When we get home, we are going to talk." She definitely never said, "Wait until your father gets home." Nah, Bruh! Nah! It was trial, jury, and punishment right then and there. No matter where we were or who was around, my mom wasn't afraid to go to town on my butt.

I can recall getting my ear pulled in the middle of the aisle at the grocery store several times. Why is it, by the way, that kids always act up in the grocery store? My mom didn't care if we were in the middle of the cereal section or the meat section. She would grab me by the ear, pull me close to her, and purse her lips while letting me know what I needed to do in order to make it out of the store safely that day. My mom had no fear of DFS (Division of Family Services), CPC (Child Protective Services), or any other organization that could take kids away. When people walked by, she didn't let up either. In those days, people didn't automatically assume a child was being abused when a parent disciplined their child. People would walk by, see my mom dealing with me and instead of offering to help me, they would offer to help her. It's like they were cheering her on or something. They reminded me of a basketball player waiting at the scorer's table to check into the game.

They were there as her backup, in case she couldn't fulfill her spanking duties for the day. Don't get me wrong, my mother didn't abuse me! Things were just different back then.

OLD TESTAMENT LAW

I would imagine things were even more different in the days of the Israelites walking through the wilderness. It was not uncommon for kids to be put to death for ill behavior in the Old Testament. Check out these Old Testament laws on the record books:

- **Exodus 21:15**–*Kids could be put to death for hitting their parents.*
- **Exodus 21:17**–*Children who dishonor their parents would be put to death.*
- **Leviticus 20:9**–*Children were to be put to death for cursing their parents.*
- **Deuteronomy 21:18–21**–*Parents who had stubborn kids who turned against them and were disobedient were required to take them to the edge of the city where they would be stoned to death. That's a harsh way to die! This was done to teach the children of the community discipline and to purge the undisciplined kids from among the good ones.*

I'm not suggesting that we put kids to death; thankfully, the Lord Jesus came to fulfill the law and show us a better way. However, the principle remains. Kids need to be taught discipline at a young age. I gave my fair share of spankings to my boys and even the little princess when they were younger.

In the back of my mind, I sometimes wondered if they were going to be upset or hold a grudge. Fortunately, that wasn't the case. They cried momentarily and certainly didn't like the punishment. However, minutes later they were climbing on my lap or ready to play some ball again. The Bible wisely teaches us to discipline our kids while they are young.[54] I believe this is because the younger they are when we discipline them, the less likely they are to hold grudges. This is yet another advantage to obeying God's Word. They will not hold it against you like they might when they are older. Try it.

2. SPORTS REQUIRED ME TO BE DISCIPLINED

As a young man, when I started to excel in sports, my football coaches were instrumental in making sure that I understood discipline and how it affected my performance. When I originally had the thought of writing about discipline for this book, I remembered many examples from my football days. As an athlete, discipline is a characteristic that is absolutely essential to success. Emotional discipline, mental discipline, and definitely physical discipline are all required in order to compete at a high level. Developing the ability to control feelings and overcome weaknesses is known as self-discipline—and all athletes need that.

Athletes have to be disciplined in their thinking in order to keep a positive winning attitude. They need discipline to stay focused in their conditioning and training. Winners don't cut corners or short change a workout. Elite athletes realize the importance of being disciplined in the way they eat, rest, and

---
54. Proverbs 19:18, NIV.

Discipline

manage their time. Discipline in the little and big things is important in every aspect of sports. Disciplined people do not give into pain, exhaustion, or any other weakness.

A person's self-discipline determines how great they will be. This is definitely true in sports and other competitions, but would also hold true in life as well. John Maxwell says that self-discipline is the ability to do what is right even when we don't feel like doing it.[55]

I'm not saying that only disciplined people will be considered successful in life. By today's standards, a successful person would be considered one who is rich and famous. The popularity of the reality TV frenzy proves that anyone can be popular and on their way to becoming rich. Others have become rich by winning the lottery or falling into money through an inheritance. It is possible to become rich and famous by accident. Have you ever heard of Kim Kardashian? She proved that anyone can become rich and famous for the wrong reasons.

However, people who follow the Kardashian family will say they have learned from other business people and have established discipline in their lives and business. Right before our eyes, we have witnessed them go from being late-night party girls to business women who operate a billion-dollar empire. Those women are wildly successful. Kim Kardashian drew criticism from an interview when she claimed the key to her

---

55. John C. Maxwell. *Talent is Never Enough: Discover the Choices that Will Take You Beyond Your Talent* (Nashville: Thomas Nelson, 2007).

success was to get up off her butt and work, although she used a little more colorful language than that.[56]

FROM GOOD TO GREAT

Fame, fortune, popularity, success–these are not true signs of greatness. Greatness puts someone in a different class than all the others around them. This can only be achieved by having discipline to do what it takes to stand above the rest. English theologian and orator Henry Parry Liddon observed, "What we do on some great occasion will probably depend on what we already are; and what we are will be the result of previous years of self-discipline." The road to greatness is realized by living a disciplined life.

Proverbs 12:1 says, "Whoever loves discipline loves knowledge." In other words, you need to learn to love discipline if you plan on being smart. Learn to love the training and correction that will produce the desired outcome that you want. Many of us love the results that discipline brings to our lives–above average intelligence, a toned body, stable finances, an even disposition. But we don't love the necessary continual training and correction along the way that it takes to achieve these results. In the words of the legendary hall of fame wrestler, Ric Flair: "Whether you like it or not, learn to love it. Woo!"

On a side note: Yes, I said Ric Flair. He's one of the greatest and most flamboyant wrestlers of all time. He is also one of my favorite wrestlers behind Hulk Hogan and The Rock. "Know your role, Jabroni!" Speaking of wrestlers, they know

---

56. Meredith Clark. "Kim Kardashian Under Fire," modified March 10, 2022, https://www.independent.co.uk/life-style/kim-kardashian-work-backlash-interview-b2032448.html

discipline. Look at their training regimen. And don't even try to tell me that it's not real. Have you ever jumped off the top of a fifteen-foot cage onto a ring covered in tacks? Yeah, that's what I thought.

Ric Flair also said, "In order to be the man, you have to beat the man." There is no point in mentioning that quote other than to show more love for the stylin', profilin', limousine-ridin', jet flyin', kiss-stealin', wheelin' n' dealin' son of a gun, Ric Flair. Woo! I digress. Yet, it takes talent to write about the wisdom of the Bible and professional wrestling in the same point. Nonetheless, living a disciplined life has other benefits aside from sports.

Weightlifters know the benefit of enduring even when they don't see the muscles forming right away. Trainers will tell us that most beginners will see noticeable muscle growth within eight weeks, while more experienced lifters will see changes in three to four weeks. We have to stay disciplined, stick with it, and be thankful for the incremental gains. We can learn to love the process and stay on the journey in order to hit your goals. People who love to work out usually seem to be on the road to greatness more than those who have to drag themselves into the gym. That's discipline; I developed this playing football.

3. FAMILY DEMANDS EXPAND THE NEED FOR DISCIPLINE

Now that I have a family of my own, with bills to pay, people to keep safe, and children to guide, I am still learning more about discipline than I imagined I would want or care to know about any particular subject. The previous two times I learned discipline were from external sources–from my mom and from football coaches in the past. That was a little easier for me to learn because I'm a natural people pleaser and I don't want to disappoint anyone. I usually like to exceed the expectations that others have of me. Therefore, it's natural for me to work hard to please the person who is teaching or training me. I've been programmed to comply with the directions and to not quit until I have exceeded all expectations. Those who have played a lot of team sports can identify with what I'm saying. We understand the power of a good coach or a strong leader.

What doesn't come naturally–and can be a problem–is trying to discipline myself. Self-discipline is internal and is perhaps the hardest to gain. However, life makes it necessary to be self-disciplined. We find discipline when we learn to deny ourself of natural, fleshly desires. We are all born with natural sinful desires and if we allow them to, they will overtake our lives and lead us down a road we don't want to be on.

As men, God has tasked us with leading our families. Before we can lead others, we must learn to lead ourselves. Lazy and disorganized people never rise to true leadership. In his book, *Spiritual Leadership,* J. Oswald Sanders said, "A leader is a person who has learned to obey a discipline imposed from without, and has then taken on a more rigorous discipline from within."[57] Your family is counting on you growing and becoming the leader they need you to be. Without you having and continuing to develop the essential quality of discipline, you won't grow into the man that God intends for you to be.

---

57. J. Oswald Sanders, *Spiritual Leadership: Principles of Excellence for Every Believer* (Chicago: Moody Press, 1994).

ASK GOD FOR WHAT YOU NEED

Are you catching this? If you need more discipline in your life, let me encourage you to ask God for it. Learn to yield your life to the Lord and surrender your will to Him. Throughout this book, you will hear me reiterate that if you are alive, God has a plan for your life. It's going to take you being filled with His Spirit and His power in order to fulfill this plan. When you are, it will be evident to those around you, especially your family, as it will be seen in the fruit you produce. Discipline will help you be more loving, kind, patient, and self-controlled.[58]

The Lord loves you so much; He only wants what's best for you. Don't make the mistake of thinking that God's discipline is a bad thing. Proverbs 3:11–12 says; "My son, do not despise the Lord's discipline and do not resent his rebuke, because the Lord disciplines those he loves, as a father the son he delights in." If you are rejecting His rebuke, running away from His reprimand, or refusing His reprove, will you just stop and allow Him to do what He wants in your life? Will you let Him?

The second definition for discipline is this: *Training expected to produce a specific character or pattern of behavior, especially training that produces moral or mental improvement.* Will you let God bring about this type of improvement to your life? He wants to and He is willing to, if you are just willing to step aside and let Him work. When you yield to God's plan and purpose for your life, you will see this type of internal discipline transform your life.

---

58. Galatians 5:22–23, paraphrased.

A LIFE WITHOUT DISCIPLINE

This whole concept of discipline is hard to learn and difficult to implement into your life. It comes with pain, displeasure, and discomfort–not to mention, it will cost time, money, and giving up your own will. The process of becoming a disciplined person is extremely difficult, yet very rewarding. Part of acting like a man means acting like a disciplined person.

What happens if you don't learn discipline and develop it in your life? The Bible says that whoever loves discipline loves knowledge, but whoever hates correction is stupid (see Proverbs 12:1, NIV). We don't like to use the word *stupid* in our family, but who am I to argue with the Bible? It also says that a spanking and a warning produce wisdom, but an undisciplined child disgraces his mother (see Proverbs 29:15, *God's Word Translation*). Men, it's our job to protect the honor of our ladies by making sure we instill discipline in our kids.

We are encouraged with the promise that a wise child accepts a parent's discipline (Proverbs 13:1, NLT). This same verse goes on to say that a mocker, or disobedient son, will refuse to listen to correction. I can't stress enough about the importance of starting to correct and train your children when they are young.

Finally, Proverbs 22:15 says that a youngster's heart is filled with foolishness, but physical discipline will drive it far away. Put another way, if you don't learn discipline, then the foolishness in your heart will eventually come out. This same verse in the *Good News Translation* says children just naturally do silly, careless things, but a good spanking will teach them how to behave. Now's a good time for all parents to say Amen.

BEFORE IT'S TOO LATE

It's so important for men to learn to become disciplined at a young age before it's too late. I tried to tell this to Cody, a young man I used to visit while he was in and out of juvenile detention. Cody was being raised by a single mom. He liked to do stupid things that would often land him in trouble at school. It wasn't long before these stupid things progressed to destructive behavior. The school realized that even at twelve years old, Cody was too much for them to handle. Having no male positive influences in their life, Cody's mom turned to me for help. At the time, I was one of the youth pastors on staff at the church that Cody only attended when his mom was able to drag him there, which wasn't very often.

On one particular occasion, I visited Cody while he was locked up for displaying wild and aggressive behavior. This time it was towards his sister. He got mad at her for something stupid and actually took a bat and hit her in the head. The police were called; he was arrested for aggravated assault and once again taken to juvenile detention. The mom asked me to pay him another visit and I did. She was afraid he was going to be permanently taken away from their home because she just couldn't handle him anymore. This wasn't his first offense and because of his undisciplined lifestyle, the judge was leaning towards giving him a strong sentence. It broke my heart because Cody was only twelve years old, but he was about to be sentenced like a grown man and would spend some serious time with his rights being stripped away–all because he didn't have self-control.

During one of my visits with Cody, I shared with him the message of Proverbs 23:14, which teaches that if we learn discipline, our soul will be saved from death. I tried to relay to him the seriousness of his actions. I told him that if he didn't learn to live a life of discipline, his youth would be wasted. We talked about how his bad and undisciplined choices would bring him nothing but a hard life and that he would most likely end up in jail for a long time. I even shared with him my own personal example of my real dad being in prison for a good portion of my life. I wanted him to understand how hard that was, not only for him, but for all of his family.

It was a tough message, but one that Cody needed to hear that day. There are so many young men, like Cody, who need us to Man UP and shoot them straight. Those who rebel against authority and scorn self-discipline will eventually find themselves paying the price. Hopefully, the price is not too high.

Chapter 9
Sacrifice

I thought I knew sacrifice–until 9/11.

September 11, 2001, is a date that our country will never forget. It's crazy to think that a whole generation is here who weren't even born when it happened. I still remember where I was. I'll never forget seeing that plane fly into the second tower on live television. Like all of us who witnessed it, that image will forever be burned into my memory.

In looking back at all the events of that day and having heard many of the stories of real-life people doing heroic things on and around that day, I can certainly say I have witnessed what sacrifice means. On that day and since, sacrifice has come to mean something new to me. When I think about all the brave men and women who courageously gave their lives to help others, it is sometimes overwhelming for me to think about. So many people Manned UP that day without giving a thought for their own safety or well-being. It was amazing!

TRUE AMERICAN HEROES

I think about all the brave firefighters who ran into the burning towers to help countless numbers of people to safety. Without a thought for their own safety, they ran up the stairs in those twin towers knowing the buildings were on fire and danger was all around them. Yet, they did this without a thought of what could happen to them. Three hundred and forty-three FDNY firefighters lost their lives while entering the burning towers. In addition, seventy-one law enforcement officers and fifty-five military personnel were also killed.[59] All were heroes.

I also think about the courageous group of men, led by passenger Todd Beamer, who gave their lives to stop another plane from crashing into the White House. Beamer and the other passengers attacked the hijackers and tried to regain control of the aircraft. They foiled the plan of the hijackers but ended up losing their lives as their plane crashed into a field in Pennsylvania. Beamer's last audible words to the other heroes who joined him to fight back were, "Are you ready? Okay. Let's roll." I first heard about their story at the ESPY (Excellence in Sports Performance Yearly) awards that year, and I was moved to tears. Pro athletes offered a standing ovation for an extended period of time and many of them were overcome, with streams of tears running down their faces.

I think about the soldiers who have lost their lives in an effort to liberate and rebuild Iraq and Afghanistan. Thousands of American soldiers have lost their lives in these wars on

---

59. Alex Finnis, INews, "How Many Firefighters Died in 9/11?," modified September 11, 2021, https://inews.co.uk/news/world/firefighters-9-11-how-many-died-emergency-workers-victims-list-september-11-attacks-1192982

Sacrifice

terror. I remember visiting the CNN website and was able to see pictures of soldiers who lost their lives. They listed all the soldiers who died and gave account of how they lost their lives.[60] Tears formed in my eyes as I scrolled through page after page. These soldiers paid the ultimate price for our country, for the world, for me. Their families have made the ultimate sacrifice too. I'm thankful to each and everyone of them.

History tells the story of countless other brave men and women who have risked–and even given–their lives for the sake of freedom throughout the years. We think of men and women who have served in the armed forces, veterans, and other soldiers. I readily think of those who died so that I can be free, but there are others, not necessarily Americans. People in other countries have paid the ultimate price so that others can experience freedom.

A SOLDIER'S LIFE

In my limited life experience, I shamefully admit that I have never truly been able to comprehend the sacrifice that many have made for my freedom. I mean, I hear about it and realize I should be thankful, but that's kind of the end of it. I don't know that I, or really, most of us, truly comprehend the sacrifice that some people make for us to be free. This wasn't a reality for me until I actually knew someone who spent time in Iraq. The Iraq war opened my eyes after seeing friends and family members being deployed to the Middle East to fulfill their tour of duty. While they were at war, we

---

60. CNN.com, http://www.cnn.com/SPECIALS/2004/oef.casualties/index.html.

were still able to enjoy so many luxuries that soldiers forfeit when they are fighting for our country.

They miss the comforts of their own home. They don't get to sit on their couch and watch their big-screen TV whenever they want. They can't go into their bathroom, take a shower or shave, or "handle their business" like most of us can. They can't walk into their pantry or open their fridge and grab some cookies, chips, or ice cream anytime they want. They don't get to fall asleep in their own bed and sleep for eight hours while their box fan keeps them cool.

Soldiers spend long periods of time away from their families. Some go months, and even years, without seeing their wife, husband, or kids. They often miss important moments in the lives of their children–the first step, the first day of school, the thirteenth birthday. My brother-in-law spent the first two years of his youngest son's life serving on military deployments. These were years spent away from his son, and those years can never be replaced.

Although they may have come home, some have sacrificed their physical or mental health and will never be the same. Many of us know soldiers who returned with serious injuries, loss of a limb, paralysis, or mental and emotional injuries. It's heartbreaking to hear that twenty-two of our warfighters commit suicide every single day.[61]

I'm thankful for organizations like The Warriors Journey whose mission it is to help heal the invisible wounds. They are a community of warriors helping warriors find true resilience. Some great organizations help warriors with the physical wounds of combat, but often the invisible wounds go

---

61. Mission 22. https://mission22.com/.

unrecognized. If you or someone you know needs help with the invisible wounds of war, contact The Warriors Journey at www.thewarriorsjourney.org.

I have also always admired The Tunnel to Towers Foundation. The Tunnel to Towers Foundation is a non-profit organization that honors the sacrifice of firefighter Stephen Siller who laid down his life to save others on September 11, 2001. They also honor our military and first responders who continue to make the supreme sacrifice of life and limb for our country.[62] It's so impressive that they are committed to providing a mortgage-free home for the families of our fallen American heroes. Every time one of their commercials comes on TV, I make it a point to stop and watch it.

FALLEN SOLDIERS

Many have even sacrificed their life, leaving behind a void for their whole family. A fallen soldier who dies on the battlefield. A sacrifice was made by more than that soldier who lost their life, but by their whole family who have sacrificed as well. These brave men and women leave behind spouses who now have to quickly adjust to raising their children by themselves. Sometimes, a fiancé, who was waiting to spend the rest of her life with her loved one, is left back home picking up the pieces. I feel for that two-year-old who will never know what her dad was like. The only memory she will have is when she looks at the picture of him holding her at the hospital the day she was born. That's sacrifice.

The dictionary definition of *sacrifice* is: "Forfeiture of something highly valued for the sake of one considered to have a

---

62. Tunnel to Towers Foundation. https://t2t.org/.

greater value or claim."[63] Calvin Coolidge said, "No person was ever honored for what he received. Honor has been the reward for what he gave." There are many American heroes who deserve our honor. May we never forget and never take their sacrifice for granted.

PAT TILLMAN

Next to the definition of the word *sacrifice* in the dictionary should be a picture of a true American hero, Pat Tillman. His story is amazing. Pat was a tremendous college football player who made it into the NFL. He played free safety at Arizona State and when he entered the NFL, began to make an immediate impact as a member of the Arizona Cardinals from 1998 until 2002. Shortly after having his best NFL season in 2000, when he broke the Cardinal's single season franchise record for tackles with 224, he announced he was going to take a break from football.

After returning from his honeymoon, he informed the Cardinals of the decision he made to place his NFL career on hold and become a U.S. Army Ranger, along with his brother. This decision shocked a lot of people and caused them to wonder why he would do such a thing. In the weeks to follow, Pat declined to speak publicly about why he made this decision. Although, his words from an interview the day after the attacks of September 11th, 2001, speak for themselves: "At times like this you stop and think about just how good we have it, what kind of system we live in, and the freedoms we

---

63. *The American Heritage Dictionary of the English Language, Fourth Edition.* (Boston: Houghton Mifflin Company, 2000).

are allowed. A lot of my family has gone and fought in wars and I really haven't done a damn thing."[64]

Pat and his brother joined the U.S. Army in July 2002, committing to a three-year term. They were assigned to the second battalion of the 75th Ranger Regiment in Fort Lewis, Washington. They served tours in Iraq during Operation Iraqi Freedom in 2003, and in Afghanistan during Operation Enduring Freedom in 2004.

Pat, along with his brother, Kevin, were recipients of the Arthur Ashe Courage Award at the 11th Annual ESPY Awards in 2003. I watched the program as they were given this award and honored by the greatest athletes in the world. I remembered thinking it was a huge deal for this guy to give up a career in the NFL to fight for our country. As a young man who once aspired to play in the NFL, I remember thinking, *He is giving up what millions of young men would do almost anything for.* I wondered what inspired him to make such a choice. Why would he give up the life and career of a professional football player to join the Army? While many admired the sacrifice; few would have made such a choice.

PAT'S SACRIFICE

In the evening of April 22, 2004, Pat's unit was ambushed as it traveled through the rugged canyon terrain of Eastern Afghanistan. His heroic efforts to provide cover for his fellow soldiers as they escaped from the canyon led to his tragic death via fratricide (the accidental killing of one's own forces in war). While the story of Pat's death may have been the most

---

64. YouTube. "Pat Tillman in His Own Words," https://www.youtube.com/watch?v=clamUNtiwrk.

publicized in the Global War on Terror, it is Pat's life, principles, and service that are his true legacy. Pat's family and friends started the Pat Tillman Foundation to carry forward that legacy by giving military service members, veterans and spouses who embody those principles the educational tools and support to reach their fullest potential as leaders, no matter how they choose to serve.[65]

I remember hearing this story on the news shortly after it happened. Several thoughts ran through my mind. I thought about the loss that Pat's newlywed wife and the rest of his family were experiencing. I thought about the heroic nature of the way in which he died. Pat signed up to serve and protect, and he lost his life doing just that. I thought about the irony of the whole situation. Some would have questioned Pat's decision to leave the NFL–where he was among the most famous and wealthy people in the world–to accept the life of the common soldier. Who would have thought he would have died in combat? The script could have played out in so many other ways. Pat's sacrifice would have been great even if he were able to finish his three years and go home to his family, possibly return back to the NFL, and live happily ever after. But the script of sacrifice called for Pat Tillman to pay an even higher price. The sacrifice cost him his life.

THE ULTIMATE SACRIFICE

This all makes me think: *Would I be able to make the same choice that Pat Tillman made?* I strive to be an honorable Christian and I'd like to think that I would, but would I? Would you?

---

65. Pat Tillman Foundation. https://pattillmanfoundation.org/the-foundation/.

SACRIFICE

As a Christian I am called to love. I am expected to love the way Christ loved; He died for the forgiveness of sins. He paid the ultimate price in His sacrifice for us. Jesus came to earth to make sure we had a way to reunite us with God through the ultimate sacrifice–His own life.

We could never live a life worthy of God on our own. So Jesus did it for us. He lived a life without sin on our behalf, becoming the ultimate sacrifice. Then He Manned UP and laid His life down, and died a painful death on the cross, so that you and I could be forgiven for our sins. That's a sacrifice of love.

In looking at the definition of the word *sacrifice*, it means to give up something highly valued for the sake of something considered to have greater value. This causes me to believe that sacrifice starts in how we view things. When we live like so many other people, believing that we are the most important people in the world, it is virtually impossible for us to sacrifice. With this mindset, we are not capable of forfeiting our own will because we don't view anything as being of greater value. This is definitely not the example that Jesus set for us. He taught us there is no greater love than "to lay down one's life for one's friends" (John 15:13, NLT).

Section 3:
Be Faithful
Walk in Obedience

- Chapter 10   Anything is Possible
- Chapter 11   Lock Your Family Up
- Chapter 12   Daddying
- Chapter 13   Helping Others

Chapter 10
Anything Is Possible

When Samuel left David's house after anointing him to be the next king of Israel, I'm certain David knew at this point–anything is possible with God. In a matter of moments, the youngest son of Jesse went from the lowly position of tending his father's sheep in the field to being anointed as the next king. The realization that he would be the one to rule over all the people of Israel, instead of any of his older brothers, couldn't have set in before the prophet finished pouring the oil over his head. God had a plan, and with Him, anything is possible.

A while later David found himself volunteering to face the Philistine champion Goliath in a death match. David wasn't even of age to join the Israelite military; yet, he was outraged that this giant would dare defy the Lord Almighty, the God of the armies of Israel. Though David knew in his heart that God would keep him safe and deliver Goliath into his hand, all the other soldiers had no idea of how unfair this fight was— for Goliath, that is! God's hand was on David and there's no way he would lose this fight. As the Philistine moved closer to attack him, David ran quickly toward the battle line to meet the giant. Reaching into his bag and taking out a stone, he slung it and struck the Philistine on the forehead. The stone sank into Goliath's forehead, and he fell face down on the ground.

So David triumphed over the Philistine with a sling and a stone; without a sword in his hand he struck down the Philistine and killed him. David ran and stood over Goliath. He took hold of the Philistine's sword and drew it from the sheath. After he killed the Goliath, he cut off the giants head with his own sword.[66]

Then David held Goliath's head real high and stuck his finger into the blood and licked it ... okay, wait. That last line isn't part of the real story; I get carried away sometimes. My bad! Nonetheless, David had no doubts, but now all of Israel knew that with God, anything is possible.

All throughout his life, time and time again, David was able to accomplish things that shouldn't have been possible by human standards. However, his life was a living testimony that with God, anything is possible. Even after his scandalous sin with Bathsheba, murdering her husband, and trying to cover it up, David was able to find forgiveness and restoration.

David demonstrates to us that with God, we don't have to be perfect or without sin. We just have to be willing to humble

---

66. 1 Samuel 17:48–51, NIV

ourselves enough to seek forgiveness when we mess up, and faithful enough to stay on the journey. This is the third part of the advice that David passed along to his son at the time of his death. He wanted Solomon to learn from his life–to be faithful and walk in obedience to God, realizing that with Him, anything is possible.

DOING THINGS THROUGH CHRIST WHO GIVES STRENGTH

Since I was a kid, Philippians 4:13 has always inspired me. It says: "I can do all this through him who gives me strength." This is perhaps my favorite verse in the Bible. Well, other than John 3:16, which is the most popular verse in the Bible and also the first verse I ever memorized.

I can remember my mother introducing Philippians 4:13 to me early on in life. When I was in third or fourth grade, shortly after she got saved, my mom started having me memorize Scripture. She felt it was important for me to hide God's Word in my heart, just as King David shared with Solomon and all the rest of us in Psalm 119:11, NIV, when he wrote, "I have hidden your word in my heart that I might not sin against you." Thus, several nights a week my mom would come into my room and we would memorize Scripture before I went to bed.

This is a practice that all parents should adopt. It's a great idea for Christian parents to get into the habit of regularly spending time in the Word with your children. It is something that will help shape their mind and spirit and will help build a foundation that will not easily be broken. I'm so thankful my mom started this with me, and this is something that I have done with all of my kids. As the priest of my home, it's my job to teach my kids how to hear the voice of God. I've started this with each of my kids, insisting they join me for daily morning devotions. The Bryant standard is that when you are old enough to read, you are old enough to read the Bible and do daily devotions.

The following are a list of verses that my mom had me memorize, and I had my kids memorize them too. If you are looking at a place to start with your kids, jump in here. I still know these Scriptures by heart; they are hidden in my heart:

- "Trust in the Lord with all your heart and lean not on your own understanding; in all your ways acknowledge him, and he will make your paths straight" (Proverbs 3:5–6, NIV).
- "For God did not give us a spirit of timidity (fear), but a spirit of power, of love and of self-discipline" (2 Timothy 1:7, NIV).
- "Be joyful always; pray continually; give thanks in all circumstances, for this is God's will for you in Christ Jesus" (1 Thessalonians 5:16–18, NIV).
- "Shout for joy to the Lord, all the earth. Worship the Lord with Gladness; come before him with joyful songs. Know that the Lord is God. It is he, who made us, and we are his; we are his people, the sheep of his pasture. Enter his gates with thanksgiving and his courts with praise; give thanks to him and praise his name. For the Lord is good and his love endures forever; his faithfulness continues through all generations" (Psalms 100, NIV).

Anything Is Possible

I could go on and on listing Scripture after Scripture that we memorized. She had me memorize the Lord's Prayer in Matthew 6, the 23rd Psalm, and the Fruit of the Spirit in Galatians 5. There are so many great Scriptures that I'm glad my mom introduced me to at an early age. I have written them on the tablets of my heart. These Scriptures have helped me walk in faithful obedience to God and I can attest their validity because I have lived them all my life.

Back to Philippians 4:13. As I said earlier, it is perhaps my favorite Scripture of them all. It speaks to me and offers a confidence that is empowering. Christ gives us strength so we can do all things. God is all powerful and wants to use us to do things. The question is: What does the "all things" consist of?

Over the course of the years, my thoughts on this verse have changed. Initially I focused on the empowerment I received to do any and all things I want to do because Christ gives me the strength. Although I believe that to be true, I now am more focused on the subject of this verse–God. My current view of this verse leads me to ask the question: "God, what are the things *You* want to do through me?" It's all about what God wants, not what we want.

I feel this verse is best understood by focusing on the things that God wants us to do. God has a plan for each of our lives. It is for the people of God to have fellowship and eternal life with Him. God's plan for you is the same: it is for you to prosper and grow spiritually in Christ. His plan to give you a hope and future has never changed. Because He wants you to be successful, He will give us the strength to fulfill His plan for our lives.

START OF MY MINISTRY

God called me into full-time ministry, and as I start my fifth decade on this earth, I'm still chasing that call. I think back to when I was about twelve years old, soon after I was called into ministry. Philippians 4:13 was the text for the first sermon I ever preached.

My family was attending Mount Calvary Church of God in Christ in Macomb, Illinois. I received an invitation to speak at a kid's crusade in one of the district churches–I believe it was in Rock Island, Illinois. In the Church of God in Christ, otherwise known as COGIC, a kid's crusade is different from what one would imagine a kid's crusade to be. In other churches, it would feature a lot of kids, puppets, games, prizes; all the typical fanfare that would draw a crowd of kids and get them excited about being in church. For some reason, I don't recall any of this at the kid's crusade I spoke at.

We had all the usual kids there whose parents made them attend church all the time. We also had a youth choir that sang two songs–an A and B selection. Of course, Mother Coleman, Mother Clark, Elder and Mrs. Starling, and all the other *honorable saints* were there–about sixty-five people in all. Then there was me; I gave the message. If memory serves, I think there were more adults in attendance at this particular kid's crusade than kids.

Nevertheless, I was asked to give the message, so I did. I toiled for weeks to prepare that sermon. Initially, I was planning to talk about obedience. I wanted to talk about how kids should obey both God and their parents. My plan was to show the benefits of living an obedient life. However, with only a couple of days left before the event, the message just wasn't coming together. I remember feeling pressured and talking with my mom about the struggles I was having. I believed that God had laid that message on my heart and I didn't understand why it wasn't coming together.

Mom advised me to relax a little and encouraged me to speak about something that I already knew. She suggested Philippians 4:13, a passage I had memorized years before, and usually referred to as one of my favorite verses. It made sense for me to speak about a passage I was familiar with, especially one that meant a lot to me. It was like a light bulb turned on in my mind.

When the day arrived, I preached my twelve-year-old heart out. The black church is known for offering immediate feedback and encouragement, so many people told me my message was "short and sweet." In retrospect, I can see they were being kind. Having now preached a few hundred more sermons, I can see how incomplete that message was. Again, I'm being kind.

Here's how it went down. First, try to imagine a twelve-year-old doing his best T. D. Jakes' impression. Back then, we didn't have video of Bishop Jakes; maybe it might have gone a little better. Or, maybe not. Now, here is pretty much the entire manuscript of my sermon:

> *"Praise the Lord, Church. Hallelujah. Turn with me in your Bibles to Philippians 4:13. While you are turning there, can somebody say, praise the Lord? The Bible says* (the COGIC church, like most black churches, used the King James Version of course): *"I can do all things, huh, through Christ, huh, which*

strengtheneth me." Hallelujah, somebody say amen. Huh. I don't think ya'll heard me. Let me say that again ... "I can do all things, huh, through Christ, huh, which strengtheneth me."

The apostle Paul is saying to me, huh, he's saying to you, huh, he's saying to us, huh...that I, huh, that you, huh, that we can do all things, huh, because God gives us the strength. Let the church say amen! Huh. This means that you (pointing my finger directly at each of the older mothers in the church) *can do all things, huh, because God gives you the strength. Hallelujah. Huh. We can do all things, huh, because God, Hallelujah, huh, gives us strength. Somebody say amen. Huh. Let the church say amen, huh.*

So that means if I want to be a preacher, hallelujah, huh, God will give me the strength, huh. If I want to be a singer, huh, God will give me the strength, hallelujah, huh. If I want to be a professional football player, huh, hallelujah, huh, God will give me His strength. Huh. Ya'll don't hear me. Huh. Somebody say amen. Huh. Whatever, huh, I said, whatever, huh, whatever I want to do; huh, God will give me His strength to do it! Huh. Say amen. Huh. Say amen. Huh. Amen."

It lasted a total of about twelve minutes and then I sat down. One minute for every year I was alive. And I don't know why I said "huh" so many times, but I knew I needed to. I wasn't sure if it was because I observed other preachers do it for dramatic effect or to fill time since I didn't have much to say. Either way, huh, I knew, huh, that I had to include a few "huhs" now and then.

This message was a bust! It was shorter than some preachers' introduction would be and it was about as shallow as the kiddy pool at the community center. I wasn't old enough to know that I should have been royally embarrassed, so at the time I was just a little embarrassed. My mom and others were affirming though, but I knew the truth in the back of my mind. I don't believe anyone there was enlightened or challenged in any special way nor was anyone impressed in the slightest bit. It would be years before I dared get back in the pulpit and attempt to do any more preaching for the Lord, who gives me strength.

WHAT IT REALLY MEANS

I realize now, that I didn't know what I was preaching. The whole point is not about what I can accomplish and then just adding Christ in there to sound biblical. The point is about what God wants to accomplish through me for His glory. In his book, *The Purpose Driven Life*, Rick Warren reminds us all that we were made for a purpose–to bring glory to the Lord through the way we live our lives. God gives each of us all the tools, the resources and the abilities we will need in order to accomplish the things He has for us to do, in order to fulfill our purpose.

In this passage, Paul is reminding the Philippians that he knows what his purpose is. He also knows that God will provide for him as he fulfills this purpose. He has learned to be content in everything because he knows he can look to the Lord for everything he will need. The things God has called him to do, he will be able to accomplish because Christ gives him strength. No one else, but Christ.

Wow! That's reassuring for us to know. God has a purpose for you and for me, for all of us. He has called us to do things for Him. Some of us will do great things for Him and some will do ordinary things for Him, but we are all called to do something for Him. Each and every one of us has a twofold purpose; to have a relationship with God and then to help as many people as possible have this same relationship with Him.

I wish I had understood this back when I preached my first sermon. That sermon would have been so much different. I still would have preached on Philippians 4:13, but I would have spent more time talking about all that God wants to accomplish in and through us. I would have encouraged people to use this strength from God to stay faithful and obedient to Him. When we, like David, spend a lifetime walking in faithful obedience to Him, we will testify that anything is possible because Christ gives us strength.

I've come to realize that I'm going to do all that God wants me to do. I can rest assured of that. If I remain faithful to Him, in my life I will accomplish everything that He wants me to do, no more, no less. That's exciting to know! Even more, there is power in knowing this. There is power that comes in knowing God's Word. This power will give you the strength to Man UP and live the life of purpose that God has called you to live.

Remember, our first purpose is to have a personal relationship with God. He desires to know each of us and have a personal relationship with each of us. If you hear nothing else in this book, hear this. God wants a personal relationship with you. Not only that, but He will give you the strength to start and maintain this relationship with Him.

Second, we are to help as many people as possible have this same type of relationship with God. A lot of people miss this part of their purpose. You know all those things that God will give you the strength to do, most of them will be used to help fulfill *this* purpose. Thousands of people die each day without having a relationship with Christ. I encourage you to Man UP and use all your skills, all of your abilities, all of your resources, all of your strength to help as many people as you can to come to know the Lord. That's what's up!

Chapter 11
Lock Your Family Up

If you google the question: "What is the biblical purpose of marriage?," here is what you'll find: "Marriage was first instituted by God in the order of creation, given by God as an unchangeable foundation for human life. Marriage exists so that through it humanity can serve God through children, through faithful intimacy, and through properly ordered sexual relationships."[67] I wasn't expecting that from google. That's a pretty good summary.

In the first two chapters of the Book of Genesis, after God finished creating everything, He looked around and said, "It's all good, baby." Well, that's how I picture it in my head anyway. Yet, after God created man (Genesis 2:18), it's interesting that

---

67. Christopher Ash, "A Biblical View of Marriage," The Gospel Coalition. https://www.google.com/search?q=what+does+the+bible+say+about+marriage&rlz=1C5CHFA_enUS843US843&oq=What+does+the+bible+say+about+marriage&aqs=chrome.0.0i512l10.5758j0j15&sourceid=chrome&ie=UTF-8.

He says, "It is not good for the man to be alone, I will make a helper that is suitable for him." I'm thankful that God created women, aren't you, guys? I'm also thankful that He affords us the blessing of finding a wife, which the Bible tells us in Proverbs 18:22 is a good thing. This same passage also tells us that after we find our wife, we will receive favor from the Lord. I believe that when we are walking in faithful obedience to God, when we are ready and properly prepared, He leads us to find a wife. He sends us out to seek our wife and once we find her, we obtain favor from the Lord.

In his book, *God at Work,* Gene Veith shared several thoughts on marriage. He said that marriage is a vocation from God. He pointed out the Reformers insisted that there is no higher or holier calling than marriage. Everything that accompanies marriage, including sexual relations, is a gift from God.[68] He goes on to say that marriage is a tangible manifestation of the relationship between Christ and the Church. This is the relationship that God most uses to demonstrate His relationship with the Church. That's why it's so important and should be preserved and revered.

Just like God offers us assurance and security in our relationship with Him, I believe men should Man UP and offer this same type of security to their lady and their family. Let me encourage you to make a deep commitment to your lady through the bond of marriage before you start to have children. This is what it means to lock your family up. Although this is very different from what culture teaches, the Bible

---

68. Gene Edward Veith, Jr., *God at Work: Your Christian Vocation in All of Life* (Crossway Books, Wheaton, IL. 2002).

teaches this to be God's standard. A locked up family puts you in a position to receive His favor and blessings.

TOO MANY ARE SHACKING UP

I've noticed that a lot of men choose not to get married, citing they aren't ready. Statistics reveal that in the past few generations, marriage is on the decline in the United States. A journal article from The National Marriage Project, University of Virginia, a study indicated that over the past fifty years, the leading marriage indicators–empirical descriptions of marriage health and satisfaction in the U.S.–have been in steady decline.[69] Over seventy-two percent of American adults were married in 1960,[70] but only fifty-three percent are married today.[71]

Statistics are even worse when it comes to men who are locking their family up and choosing to have babies with the woman they are married to. In 1970, just a couple of years before I was born, eighty-nine percent of all births were to married parents.[72] Today, just fifty short years later, recent estimates show that about forty percent of births in the United States occur outside of marriage.[73] Sadly, in the black community, the numbers are even more devastating; in

---

69. W. Bradford Wilcox, Editor. "The State of Our Unions: Marriage in America" (The National Marriage Project, University of Virginia, 2009).
70. The Marriage Index. Hampton University, 2009. Institute for American Values and the National Center on African American Marriages and Parenting.
71. Pew Research Center, Marriage and Cohabitation in the U.S.
72. The Marriage Index. Hampton University, 2009. Institute for American Values and the National Center on African American Marriages and Parenting.
73. Elizabeth Wildsmith, Jennifer Manlove, Elizabeth Cook."Dramatic Increase in Percentage of Births Outside Marriage," https://www.childtrends.org/publications/dramatic-increase-in-percentage-of-births-outside-marriage-among-whites-hispanics-and-women-with-higher-education-levels.

any search in the past decade, nearly three out of four black babies are brought into this world without both a mother and father in the home. The ramifications of this is devastating to our community.

It appears that too many men believe they have to have it all together and live as perfect saints in order to get married and lock their family up. That's just not the case. Marriage is two flawed people coming together to create a space of stability, love, and consolation–a "haven in a heartless world," as Christopher Lasch describes it.[74] Then, each of them chooses to mutually submit to each other and do their best to serve one another, just like Christ gave himself up to serve the Church.

In his book, *The Meaning of Marriage,* Tim Keller talks about the "Great Secret of Marriage." The secret is found in Ephesians 5:25 when Paul said: "Husbands, love your wives, just as Christ loved the church and gave himself up for her." Keller says the "secret" is not simply the fact of marriage per se. It is the message that what husbands should do for their wives is what Jesus did to bring us into union with himself. And what is that? Jesus gave himself up for us.[75]

SPEAK YOUR SPOUSE'S LOVE LANGUAGE

One way that I strive to give myself up for my wife is to learn to speak her love language. This concept has changed my marriage and my life when it comes to relationships with other people. I had for some time in my adult years been aware of the concept of loving people the way in which they

---

74. Christopher Lasch. *Haven in a Heartless World: The Family Besieged* (New York, Basic Books, 1977).
75. Tim Keller, *The Meaning of Marriage: Facing the Complexities of Commitment with the Wisdom of God* (Random House, New York, NY. 2011).

understand and receive that love. It wasn't until after I had been married for a couple of years that I was formally introduced to the book, *The Five Love Languages,* by Gary Chapman. There are five love languages: Words of Affirmation, Acts of Service, Receiving Gifts, Quality Time, and Physical Touch. Chapman's premise is that each gift is important and expresses love in its own way. Learning your partner's and your own primary love language will help create a stronger bond in your relationship.[76]

The book goes into great detail about loving others, mainly your spouse, in a way they understand and appreciate. Chapman also introduces the concepts of continuing to make deposits into your spouse's love tank. Making deposits consists of showing love to your spouse or loved one over and over so that they have the feeling of knowing that you truly love them.

It's important to make these emotional deposits into our spouse's love tank, because on a day-to-day basis we do bone-headed things that hurt our spouse or annoy them. In essence, we are making withdrawals from our spouse's love tank. It's easy to make a withdrawal. Oftentimes, we don't even have to work on making a withdrawal, and sometimes we don't even know we did. Because of the time we spend with our loved ones in close proximity and because our natural sinful nature is very selfish and rude, we often do and say things that hurt our spouse.

My wife and I experienced a rough couple of years when we were first married. We have been close friends since high

---

76. Gary Chapman, *The Five Love Languages: How to Express Heartfelt Commitment to Your Mate* (Chicago, IL: Northfield Publishing, 1992).

school and have known each other since grade school. We have been in each other's lives for a long time and have seen the good, the bad, and the ugly. We have always kept it "real." We feel free to say pretty much anything we are thinking and talk about every part of each other's lives. Because of this close friendship, when we were first married, it was easy for us to say things to each other that were considered offensive and oftentimes hurtful, without even realizing it. We were both making constant withdrawals from each other's love tank.

After a short while of this and by the grace of God, we discovered Gary Chapman's concepts of the love languages. It has strengthened our marriage and given us tools to use in growing our marriage in the Lord. I was first introduced to the book in a Sunday school class for young married couples, although I believe Angie had heard of the book before. I was immediately interested and intrigued. The book and the love language concepts began to positively influence my life immediately. I first studied the love languages to learn them, and then I committed to living them in my family and my life.

The purpose of this chapter is not to talk about how well I know the love languages; you can gain that knowledge by reading the book yourself. Although I will offer a brief introduction of the love languages, I mainly want to talk about what the book means to me and how it has impacted my life, specifically my marriage. I feel it necessary for me to share the love languages so that you will have some idea as to what I am talking about when I refer to them. Also, I would recommend reading the book for yourself and studying the love languages. It's important to know your language for giving and receiving love, and also to be able to recognize the love language of your spouse and other loved ones.

I'M FLUENT IN SPEAKING MY WIFE'S LOVE LANGUAGE

The most important love language to me personally is the giving and receiving of gifts. You would think it's most important to me because this is my primary love language, but you would be wrong. It's most important to me because this is my wife's primary love language. My wife loves (and I mean *loves*) to receive gifts. She likes to receive big gifts, little gifts, gifts on special days–Christmas, birthdays, and Valentine's Day–*"just because"* gifts, unexpected gifts, and even expected gifts. She likes gifts that are inexpensive that are offered regularly, and she likes expensive gifts that come every now and then.

When I give her something, it shows her that I have been thinking about her. It doesn't really matter what I give her as long as there is a good reason behind it. Now, don't get me wrong. I have missed the mark on a gift to her in the past, and she isn't afraid to let me know either. I have heard the words: "What were you thinking? Do you even know me?," more than I care to admit.

I don't want to offer the impression that Angie is ungrateful or unappreciative, because she is very grateful for the gifts I give her. The reactions she sometimes offers are not her reactions to the particular gift I have given her, but to the level of thought I did or did not give in choosing the gift. Angie believes in such a thing as the perfect gift for every occasion. She believes that it starts with knowing the person and thinking of them and what they want or would like. When I give her the right gift, it shows her that she is the most important person to me at that time. She feels like I was thinking about her and this makes her feel special. I know her and have paid attention to her wants and desires.

I give gifts on a regular basis to love Angie in her love language. Talk about pressure! After all these years, I now realize my wife's primary love language and I do my best to speak it on a regular basis. I've been told often that knowing is half the battle. It's a constant struggle for me to put into action that which I know. Isn't that the way it goes in life though? The things we know to do, we don't do. And all the things we don't want to do, we do.[77] The Bible mentions this in the writings of Paul. This struggle is definitely true in marriage.

I encourage you to learn to speak the primary love language of your spouse, then speak it often. It's going to take a lot of practice, determination, and hard work, but you can do it! Do you know your spouse's love language? Here are some things to think about that could help you figure it out:

1. *If your spouse's primary love language is **quality time**, make it a priority to spend blocks of quality time with her, enjoying each other's company.*
2. *If her primary love language is **physical touch**, learn to touch her in the right spots at the right time. This will show her the affection that she needs. If you are single and you are reading this, skip ahead to love language #3. I don't want to get you all excited or*

---
77. Romans 7:15–20

excite your feelings of love before the right time.[78] *You know what I'm sayin'?! But fellas, this is something we need to work on. We all know that men have needs– again, you know what I'm talking about! But women have needs too. When you learn to take care of your spouse's needs for affectionate physical touch, she will then take care of your needs. You smell what I'm cookin'?! Trust me, I know what I'm talking about. I have five kids. My wife can't keep her hands off me.*

3. *If your spouse's primary love language is* **words of affirmation,** *make it a habit to speak uplifting and positive words to her. I believe we should do this anyway with everyone, but especially so if this is your spouse's primary love language. In today's cynical world, this isn't easy to do. The model we see is that people make millions of dollars with their sarcastic humor. It's easy to adopt this way of communicating with our friends and loved ones. Truth be told, this type of humor and communication is not healthy and is very dangerous for your relationship. Learn to offer words of affirmation to your spouse especially if this is their primary love language.*

4. *If* **acts of service** *are your spouse's primary love language, then you need to "man down," grab that apron, and do some housework. Sorry, man! But hey, you gotta do what you gotta do to show love to your spouse. Look for and do the nice little unexpected things to show you care. Help around the house, watch the kids so she can have a moment to herself, fill her car up*

---

78. Song of Solomon 3:5, paraphrase of New Century Version

> with gas, cook the occasional meal. Whatever she likes for you to do in order to serve her and show her you love her.
> 5. **If giving and receiving gifts** is your spouse's primary love language, take it from me, get a second job. Kidding, not kidding. This love language takes a little extra thought and the proper planning. You have to remain on your game all year around looking for opportunities to give that special and unexpected "just because" gift. It's these type of gifts that score the most points and will lead to a lot of love language #2 being practiced. Holla if you hear me!

Regardless of your spouse's primary love language, get in the habit of regularly speaking it and showing your spouse that you love and cherish her. So, start right away by identifying how she wants to be loved and then love her that way.

Manning UP in this area is perhaps the most important area of life. Truth is, no more important relationship exists in your life that you need to ensure you are displaying the right behavior towards than your wife. In over twenty-seven years of marriage, I have come to realize that what they say is true: "If Momma ain't happy, ain't nobody happy!"

If you've been paying attention, you will notice that faith is a big part of my life in every area, including marriage. My faith has taught me to put God first in every area of my life, and the wisdom of my years has taught me this is especially true when it comes to marriage. We can't look for our spouse to fill up our love tanks in a way that only God can. When we do this, we are setting ourselves up for failure and asking for something that is impossible. It's important for us to walk in faithful obedience to God and seek to stay in right relationship with Him. Obedience brings blessings. We will go into more detail about this concept later, but be encouraged that this includes the blessing of a good and healthy marriage.

Chapter 12
Daddying

*Being a good dad means
being there for your kids–all the time!*

I never wanted to be a *baby's daddy!* I grew up watching most of the men I knew have this title: baby's daddy. I didn't want that! I wanted to be a father–one who was actively involved in his kids' life and modeled loving their mother. I believe many men want this; however, we are not always willing to do what it takes to acquire the title we want. So, we settle for titles that come from giving in to our fleeting sexual desires. I get it, I understand the strong sexual urges and desires of a young man. So many beautiful women, and so little time. I get it. However, that mindset is why we have so many baby daddies running around. We have to make some changes–that's what the songwriter Tupac said.[79] There's gotta be a better way!

---

79. "Changes" lyrics © 1992 Universal Music–Z Songs, Universal Music Corp., Back On Point Music, Amaru Publishing, Zappo Music, Universal Music Z Songs.

The Bible teaches us that husbands and wives are to satisfy each other sexually.[80] Their bodies do not belong just to themselves, but also to the other person. The wife's body belongs to the husband, and the husband's body belongs to the wife. Think about that for a moment. How freeing and how liberating would your relationships be when you realize that the Bible offers clear teaching and instruction on such an important topic. I think it's fair to say that God wants you to have sex and a lot of it! Good sex! However, He intends for you to do it within the confines of the relationship standards that He has set out for you. He tells husbands and wives to not deprive one another of sex except when both agree to devote themselves to prayer, and even then, it should only be for a limited time. After that, they should come together again and continue to satisfy each other sexually.[81] In his teaching on sexual relations, Gene Veith said: "This sexual freedom within marriage is very different–and far more liberating–than today's secular attitudes toward sex"!

Something may be good when done inside a vocation, but bad when it is done outside that vocation. Sex outside of marriage is wrong, but not because there is anything wrong with sex. Within the vocation of marriage, it is a great good; one of God's best inventions. Can I get an amen? However, outside of the vocation of marriage, sex is considered a sin, and therefore, wrong. To be extremely clear, God does not intend for you to have sex with anyone other than your spouse. Veith goes on to say: "You have no authority to have this positive physical relationship with someone you are not married

---

80. 1 Corinthians 7:13, NIV.
81. 1 Corinthians 7:5, NIV.

to. There is a good reason why there must be a vocation to have sex: By its nature and its purpose, sex leads to another vocation, that of parenthood."

LOOK HOW GREAT MY KIDS ARE

The more time I spend with my kids, the more I realize how much I love them and how important they are to me. It's hard for people without kids to understand this. Before I had kids, some of my friends with kids would talk about them all the time. I wasn't the least bit interested in what their kids were doing in school or at home, so it was pretty annoying. They would tell all kinds of stories about the funny, frustrating, or even annoying things their kids would do. I remember thinking that when I did finally have kids, I would never bore people with these kinds of stories.

One of my coworkers in particular would come to work almost every day with a story about the supposedly hilarious things his kids did the night before. Every now and then he had an interesting story, but for the most part, I couldn't help but wonder why he was wasting all of our time and the company's money telling me stories about his kids. Did he really think I wanted to know that his youngest kid threw his wife's hairbrush in the toilet, or that his oldest kid scored two goals in his 4th grade rec-league soccer game? I almost resented him for talking about his kids so much. I vowed that when I had kids, I would never do this. I was determined to not infringe on people's time with stories about my kids, no matter how interesting I thought the stories to be.

Little did I know this would soon change when we started having kids. I feel I need to take this time to apologize to all the high school and college students, all the co-workers and employees, and all of my friends, who throughout the years have had to listen to endless stories about my totally wonderful and extraordinary kids. I'm so sorry for subjecting you to these stories that I, as their parent, thought were funny and exciting, but now realize you could actually have cared less about. I also want to say thank you for appearing to be genuinely interested and for acting as though you really cared. Many of you have fooled me pretty well. Thank you!

Nevertheless, in spite of not wanting to hear my coworker's endless stories, I will admit that I admired him for being the kind of father who was very involved in the lives of his children. Looking back, I realize I learned a lot from the example he set, without even knowing he was mentoring me in fatherhood. His stories demonstrated love in the form of patience towards his kids. He was good at letting kids act their age and giving them room to just be kids. Although I only witnessed it from afar, he seemed to be the type of dad who would work through problems and dilemmas with his kids. He wasn't the type of dad who would sit on the sidelines and criticize everything without offering advice and correction as to how to improve. I appreciated this about him, although this style of parenting was completely different from the way I was raised. In time, I came to admire him for being an attentive and engaged father.

In my own life, although I loved and respected him, my stepdad wasn't much of a talker. But he was the only real father I knew. He grew up in the generation when the primary role for fathers was to provide for and protect their kids. Although he didn't often have much to say, when he did speak, I knew to listen up and do what he said. In retrospect, he taught more by what he did, by the way he lived his life, and the example he set to work hard and overcome obstacles.

I learned from him that acting like a man had more to do with behavior than words spoken. His way was not to just say you were a man, but to make sure you acted like you were a man. He modeled that, in regards to our kids, our wives, our moms, our sisters, and all others, certain things were expected of us as men. We learned to acknowledge this, figure out what is expected of us, then deliver. I learned from my dad's example, the example of my coworker, and others, and have come to realize that although it may look different, fathers need to show up and be present for their kids.

WHAT DOES "BEING THERE" FOR YOUR KIDS MEAN?

Quite simply, it means being there!–spending time with them. Don't have kids that you can't raise. Don't be a "baby's daddy!" Don't let your kids grow in this world without having a relationship with their father. Kids need to see their father every day and spend quality time with him–daily. They need to see their father loving their mother! They need to see the example of a man changing diapers, even the dirty ones. They need their dad to kiss their "ouchies," help with homework, and attend their school events. I can't imagine someone else teaching my kids how to throw and catch a ball.

One of my greatest earthly joys is that of being a father. Who knew it would be so rewarding? I was there for the first steps of each of my kids and made sure my little princess didn't fall too hard when she was learning to walk. Hey, boys are a dime a dozen in my family, but I only have one little baby girl. It is what it is! I remember the first day we signed our oldest son Trey up for his first basketball league. He was so excited, but I'll admit, I was even more. We left that gym with all smiles. As soon as we arrived home, Trey moved his little basketball hoop into the garage so he could have more room to practice.

Even though it was the dead of winter, he stayed in the garage practicing for three days straight, so he could get a jump on the competition. I was there with him the whole time. I remember him asking if I would be his coach. I was so elated that my boy wanted me to be around and coach his team.

I did have to decline the offer of being the coach, however, because someone had to run both cameras and the camcorder and I didn't think Ang could handle all of the equipment by herself while I was on the sideline. I certainly wasn't about to take the chance of not having this footage documented on all three recording devices; the regular camera, video camera, and digital camera. You can never have too much footage. I just knew that one day ESPN would come asking for pictures and video footage for the "Beyond the Glory" story they would do on Trey once he made it into the Basketball Hall of Fame. I would be there for every moment and I wanted to be prepared.

Another way I spent time with my kids when they were young was at bedtime. I made it a priority and considered it a privilege to put them to sleep pretty much every night. The boys shared rooms with each other so that was easy, but when Katie came along, because she was the only girl, she was the only one in the family who never had to share a room. As well, considering that she was the youngest, before I retired from laying on bedroom floors, I spent many nights on her floor while she fell asleep. I loved this tradition that started when Trey was a baby and I carried all the way until Katie was old enough not to need me there.

Bedtime was often the best time of the day for me. I remember stealing kisses from my boys after they fell asleep in my arms. I would kiss them over and over, telling myself that it had to be the last one so that I didn't wake them. One more usually meant that I would stop kissing them after five or six kisses. Even though they were fast asleep, I wanted them to know they were loved.

As the boys grew older and moved from cribs to toddler beds, the bedtime routine got even more fun with the discovery of air tents. For a while, Trey and Michael wanted to make air tents every night. But this big offensive line brotha couldn't lay on the hard floor every night, so Ang suggested we make air tents on Tuesdays, Thursdays, and Saturdays only. Well, Josh and Mason felt they weren't getting enough air tent time so we added a few more nights to the rotation, every Sunday night and, of course every holiday was a perfect night for an air tent.

Oh, wait! It just occurred to me that some of you may not know what an air tent is. You can make an air tent by taking a box fan, setting it up at one end of the floor, and putting a flat sheet over the top, creating an air bubble inside that you lay in. Oh, and an air tent wasn't an air tent without sneaking animal crackers and cream cheese icing inside without mom noticing. My son Mason discovered that the best air tents were made at our house in Kansas City. Our living room was big enough that we could position the couches at the edge of each side and create the perfect air pocket. This discovery made it more fun so we had to expand air tent nights to also include most Mondays and Wednesday nights when I was home from church early.

By the time Katie came along, with the two other little boys still around, we also discovered that air tents were viable at nap time as well. However, Katie would continually get up and move around, causing the top sheet to fall down. This always caused Josh and Mason to scream, "Katie!" After this happened a couple times, it wasn't long before Ang would come out and declare it was time for the kids to go down for a real nap.

The kids and I came to conclude that pretty much anytime was a good time to make an air tent. Those were special times! I miss them. I wouldn't trade those times for anything in the world, and sometimes wish we could make another air tent, just for old times' sake. Alas, the kids are all too big and I'm way too old. I'm at the age where it has to be a "high pile" shag carpet with extra padding underneath before I try to put these old knees on the floor.

I credit this quality time I spent with my kids when they were young as an investment that paid off when they got older. I'm so blessed that at every stage in life my kids were always willing to spend time with me. Going for bike rides, going to the movies, hanging out at home playing cards or board games, or dropping everything and taking a last minute road trip to see our beloved Chicago Bears play, we've spent a lot of quality time together and made a lot of lasting memories.

None of those memories would have happened if I hadn't been committed to being there for my kids.

Make it a priority to be there for your kids, too. Be intentional about spending time with them, having fun, loving them, and just enjoying each other. In his book, *Bringing Up Boys,* Dr. James Dobson says that children of all ages, both male and female, have an innate need for contact with their fathers. He says that boys suffer most from the absence or non-involvement of fathers.

Even after spending five decades on this earth and as the father of four boys of my own, this hits home with me. I know what it's like to not have your my real dad in my life. Dr. Dobson goes on to say that boys are troubled today primarily because their parents, and especially their dads, are distracted, overworked, harassed, exhausted, disinterested, chemically dependent, divorced, or simply unable to cope. Chief among our concerns is the absence of the masculine role modeling and mentoring that a dad should be providing.[82] That's an indictment on us men. Let's not let that be said of us.

"BEING THERE" MEANS SETTING A POSITIVE EXAMPLE

If you were to google what it means to set a positive example, here's what you would find: "To do something or act in a way others will or should emulate; to act as a positive model for others."[83] If there were a picture of an example setter in the dictionary, you would find the picture of a parent. We are

---

82. Dr. James Dobson. *Bringing Up Boys: Practical Advice and Encouragement for Those Shaping the Next Generation of Men* (Wheaton, IL: Tyndale House Publishers, 2001).
83. *The Free Dictionary.* "Set a good example," https://www.thefreedictionary.com/.

our kids' first and most important teachers. The people they will spend the most time with, forming and shaping who they become.

Proverbs 22:6 teaches us that it's a parent's job, or vocation, to train up a child in the way they should go. We are the first example they see, the ones responsible to teach them God's Word.[84] As men, we shouldn't leave this important responsibility to our child's mom. Statistics show that only thirty-four percent of all children in America will live with both biological parents through the age of 18, so a lot of kids are missing out on the influence of fathers in their life.[85] This is not the way God intended it to be. Kids need constant guidance, supervision, and direction in their lives before they become young adults. With so much work to be done to shape them, it takes both parents actively engaged in their lives.

The number one job of parents is to teach their kids how to hear the voice of God and respond accordingly. Part of the way parents assume this responsibility is to see that their children are raised in church. Teach your kids to hear the voice of God for themselves. The primary way we hear God's voice is through reading His Word, the Bible. Set this example for your kids by letting them see you read it, then teach them to do it for themselves. This is absolutely a great place to start in setting an example for your kids.

The Bible tells us to be doers of the Word and not just be hearers.[86] Show your kids how to be obedient to God's Word so they will be in a position to receive God's blessings. I make it a point to talk with my kids about developing discipline in

---

84. Deuteronomy 4:9, NIV.
85. Dr. James Dobson. *Bringing Up Boys*.
86. James 1:22, NIV.

their lives, and I talk about how this is possible when they fill their hearts and minds with God's Word. This is possible for you and your kids with God's help.

Strive to be a positive example for your kids emotionally, spiritually, socially, etc. Be present and engaged in their lives so they see the example you set for them in all things. Kids need to have role models. In today's society it's disappointing that no one wants to accept this responsibility. When you make the choice to have kids, you are making the choice to be a role model. It is your responsibility to teach your kids how to act and respond in every situation they may face in life.

LEADERS ARE READERS

Help your kids understand the importance of being lifelong learners. Teach them that leaders are readers. This means that you should learn to be a reader too. I make it a goal to read at least three books every month, so I prioritize spending time reading. Don't adopt the mindset that many have by saying you don't like to read. By spending time reading and learning, you will be a model for your kids for how to grow intellectually. Be an example of a person who is continuously learning so your kids will see what you do and do the same.

As a young father, I didn't understand how much my boys would watch me. Now that I have a little girl, I'm surprised at how much she watches me too, and tries to do and say everything that I do. It's kind of cool and kind of nerve-racking at the same time. From the jokes I tell, to the attitudes I have, to the way I treat their mother and other people, even to the way I enter the bathroom with a book in my hand, my kids are always watching to see if my actions match my words.

Understand that your kids will be watching you too. They want and need to see men who are wise and honest, and strive to grow and improve all the time.

We don't have to take very many trips around the sun before we realize that life is hard. Things happen, problems arise, failure is inevitable, and we all experience loss at some point along the way. One of the best things a father can do is teach his kids how to work through emotions so that they will continue to engage in society appropriately. Be purposeful in modeling this for your kids and learn to consistently coach your kids about how to grow and mature socially.

Dr. William Pollock, Harvard psychologist and author of *Real Boys*, believes that fathers are crucial in helping kids, especially boys, manage their emotions. He says without the guidance and direction of a father, a boy's frustration often leads to varieties of violence and other antisocial behavior.[87] Talk about problems openly and freely. At age appropriate times, trust your kids enough to talk about your problems too. If you consistently and faithfully model this for your kids, they will follow you and learn from your conversations.

The family that I lead lives very differently from the way that I grew up. I don't remember our family being very open in dealing with problems. My parents were old school, often ending conversations with the old proverbial, "Because I said so!" I have noticed that in many black families, problems usually are not open for discussion. They don't get much dialogue about issues that affect the kids or the family. Whatever mom and dad says is usually just the way it goes.

---

87. William Pollock, *Real Boys: Rescuing Our Sons from the Myths of Boyhood* (New York: Henry Holt and Company, 1998).

I've come to realize that when we make space available for open discussion, kids learn to process things better and are prepared to make good decisions down the road. When parents openly discuss their problems and bravely work through their own emotions, they set the foundation for their children to learn to do the same. When we have the courage to do this, we set a wonderful example for our children that hopefully fosters open communication in their own relationships down the road. I've seen that cultivating this type of culture in our family has opened the door for me to be able to speak into my kids' life and offer advice on key things as they have grown older.

"BEING THERE" MEANS WORKING TO LOCK YOUR FAMILY UP

Being there for your kids means having a good family situation. I fundamentally believe that having a mom and dad who love each other and demonstrate this love for their children is one of the best blessings children can receive.

Scripture teaches that husbands are to love their wife just like Christ loved the Church and gave himself up for her.[88] This passage gives us a picture of a man who sacrifices himself–his wants, his needs, his strength, his very life if it comes to that–for the good of his woman. Veith said:

> "If marriage mirrors the relationship between Christ and the Church, with the husband in Christ's role, then the husband ought first to give himself up for the wife, whereupon in response the wife, playing the part of the

---

88. Ephesians 5:25, NIV.

Church, will respond by submitting to his good intentions for her."

If you are like me and your goal is to not be a baby daddy, then do things the way that God intended and lock your family up. Man UP and do what Beyoncé said: if you like it, then put a ring on it!

Until you are ready to make this type of faithful commitment to a lady, I suggest you keep your pants zipped. I know this is hard to hear, some would even say it's ridiculous to expect people to abstain from sex until marriage. *That's way too old fashioned,* they may be thinking. I would say that's why we have too many kids being born into single parent families. I never wanted to be a baby's daddy because I wanted a strong close family. So for the young men reading this without kids, keep your pants zipped. That's a message you won't hear a lot about. Learn to obey the Lord's commands concerning sexuality.

President Barack Obama consistently promoted strong families, specifically in the African-American community. In a 2013 speech, in Chicago's Hyde Park, he talked about fatherhood and his own upbringing as the son of a single mother.[89] In 2008, while he was still Senator Obama, in a Father's Day speech at the Apostolic Church of God in Chicago, he gave some alarming statistics. He said, "We know the statistics —that children who grow up without a father are five times more likely to live in poverty and commit crime; nine times more likely to drop out of school, and twenty times more

---

89. *USA Today,* "Obama Speaks on the Importance of Fatherhood," https://www.usatoday.com/story/theoval/2013/02/17/obama-chicago-fatherhood-economy-gun-control/1925727/, accessed April 1, 2023.

likely to end up in prison."⁹⁰ Hearing these statistics brings two things to mind; 1) it's a tough road for kids without a dad, and 2) don't let someone else raise your kids. Being a parent–being a dad–is a full-time job. You can't just be a dad on the weekends only.

To the young man who is a baby daddy right now, make the decision to be the best father to the kids you have. Be there for them in every way–emotionally, socially, physically, and spiritually. But make the decision to not have more kids until you are married. Even consider locking your family up with the baby's momma, if that's an option. It may take some mentoring or counseling for you to become the husband and father you need to be, but it'll be worth it.

To the man who is already a father and married to your kids' mother–good for you. Keep going. Continue to work on your relationship with your lady. As I mentioned before, loving your wife is one of the best things you can do to provide a stable home for your children. Decide to put God at the center of everything you do from here on out.

In a Father's Day sermon, pastor and author T.D. Jakes said that everything begins with fatherhood. It all began with God the Father and ends with Him, from Genesis to Revelation, everything poured out of Him.⁹¹

LOVING YOUR WIFE

The best way to be there for your kids is to raise them in a loving family where you are modeling what it means to

---

90. Politico. "Text of Obama's Fatherhood Speech," https://www.politico.com/story/2008/06/text-of-obamas-fatherhood-speech-011094, accessed April 1, 2023.
91. YouTube. T.D. Jakes' sermon "Real Men Pour In," June 19, 2022, https://www.youtube.com/watch?v=4fTg4FHSSQY accessed April 1, 2023.

love and honor their mother. Take the time to work on your marriage relationship and show your kids how to have a successful marriage. Anyone who has been married for more than two years and has made it past the honeymoon stage completely realizes that marriage is hard. As I previously said, statistics show that most marriages end in divorce. For you and me, it doesn't have to be this way. God intended for a family to be made up of a mother, a father, and their children. Work to keep it this way. It may be difficult, but you can have a loving and successful marriage.

Pastor and author Craig Groeschel, in his book *WEIRD*, challenges us to tend the garden of our marriage. He says normal people neglect their marriage and expect it to thrive. He goes on to say if you want to buck the norm and have what few have, do what you do–concentrate on your marriage as a living, growing garden that requires planting and tending, watering and weeding.[92] That bears repeating: if you want to buck the norm and have what few have–a healthy marriage that is blessed and fulfilling–do what few do. Man UP and faithfully and consistently work on your marriage.

I wish I could give you five simple steps to achieving and maintaining a great marriage, but I can't. I don't even know that anything like this exists. However, I can tell you from personal experience that, although being married is one of the greatest accomplishments of my life, it takes a lot to make it work. A good marriage consists of such buzzwords as *commitment, faithfulness, compromise, determination, selflessness, patience, kindness, gentleness, self-control,* and *forgiveness.*

---

92. Craig Groeschel, *WEIRD: Because Normal Isn't Working* (Grand Rapids, MI: Zondervan, 2011).

Honestly, that list could go on and on. Nonetheless, you can have a good marriage, but you have to always continue to work at it. Work on your marriage not only for the sake of you and your spouse, but for the sake of your children too.

Now that I am a father, I can't imagine not spending time with my kids. Early on in our marriage, my wife was adamant about starting our own family traditions. Now I'm so thankful for this. She helped me see how special these traditions would be as our kids got older. I am so thankful that when they were toddlers, most nights I took the time to engage in the bedtime routine. When I was home, I was happy to be the one to put them to sleep. My wife was home with them, tending to them most of the day, so it was my high honor to handle bedtime. I started a fun nighttime routine with Trey that I managed to continue all the way through to when Katie wanted her own time to read at night.

My routine with the kids was our own, and it special to us. It started with us going to their room, saying our prayers, and then the fun began. We sometimes would lay on the floor and build the aforementioned air tent. Other times we would end up in a wrestling match. With the boys, wrestling usually involved stripping down to nothing but our underwear. It was Dad vs. the "Underwear Puncher Guys," as Michael named themselves. We had fun and epic matches to wind down before going to sleep. Ang, however, didn't always see it this way. She would often hear the commotion and come in and point out that I was actually not helping them wind down; in fact, I was doing quite the opposite. I did my best to make memories and have a good time while the windows of their hearts were open. Night time was always a fun tradition for me and the kids.

MEMORIES THAT LAST A LIFETIME

As I was finishing writing this chapter, I popped my head in Mason's room to say goodnight. He noticed I was hidden away in my office writing most of the day. I told him I was finishing the chapter on air tents. We had a few good laughs as we reminisced on his favorite times spent in the air tent, with the animal crackers and icing. They were some great times! I can't imagine not having had these special times with my kids. We created memories that all of us will carry with us throughout our lifetimes.

I've heard it said that when raising kids, sometimes the days seem to drag on forever, but the years fly by. It seems like just a few short months ago, I was watching Michael take his first few steps. What a sight to see that little tyke wobble around the house and fall down every few steps. Then just a little while later, I watched him walk around the house looking for things to get into. It was then, and it still is now, my job to keep him out of things that may cause trouble for him or for us. I loved watching him explore our house looking for new things to get into then, and I like seeing him spread his wings now, looking for new areas of the country to explore. One thing has stayed the same, he puts everything in his mouth. It was toys, remote controls, dog food, or anything off the ground back then, but it's all kinds of food now.

Random question: why do kids do that? They put anything in their mouth when they are little and they put all the food in the house in their mouth when they get older. Nevertheless,

I can't imagine not being around for any of these memorable times in his life. Or any of my other kids for that matter. There's no way I would feel like a dad by sending their mother a check at the end of the month while she took care of them. This is not the situation any father should accept for his family, if he can at all avoid it.

Daddying is the result of choices that you make before any kid arrives. When you choose to fool around outside of the sanctity of marriage, you are making the choice to possibly be on the "baby's daddy" list. I encourage you to Man UP and make wise choices right now that will affect your future. When you finally decide you are ready to have kids, have them the way God intended–within the confines of marriage to a wonderful lady who will faithfully work alongside you to build your beautiful God-honoring family.

Chapter 13
Helping Others

Help enough people get what they want and eventually you will get what you want.
                    –Zig Ziglar

I don't usually remember times and dates, however June 2006 stands out so clearly in my mind. We had just moved to Fort Myers, Florida, to take a ministry position and, just across Alligator Alley, Shaq was finishing up his second season with the Miami Heat. It was an exciting time for Southwest Florida and for me personally because I'm a huge Shaq fan. He was about ready to lead the Heat to an NBA championship in only his second year in Miami, and so quickly after his public feud with Kobe–who I blame for ruining that dynamic relationship–which led to Shaq being run out of Los Angeles. Team Shaq all the way!

One night in particular I was enjoying watching the Heat lay the smack down on Dirk Nowitzki and the Dallas Mavericks.

There I was sitting in my air-conditioned living room, watching my cable television on my 50-inch Toshiba big-screen TV. I had just finished eating a snack, after having a wonderful meal that my wife prepared for our family earlier that evening. We had plenty left over too, so much that I remember looking forward to eating that delicious meal again the next day for lunch.

During halftime of the game, I decided to flip through the channels for a few minutes to see what else was on. I landed on an interview that Anderson Cooper was having with Angelina Jolie. I never had a problem with Anderson Cooper, but I've never been a huge Angelina Jolie fan. Yet, I was drawn in and wanted to hear what she had to say.

As I watched that interview, I was surprised that she was talking about people suffering all around the world and how she was working to show them compassion. I wasn't expecting that, not from her, and not during the NBA Finals. But I was moved to the point of tears as I sat there watching her share. In those few short minutes, Angelina Jolie did an extremely effective job of bringing attention to the over 15 million refugees around the world that had been displaced because of wars and famine. Many of them were women and children, and most of them were without enough food to survive more than a couple of days.

I know this is a book for men, but I'm not ashamed to say that I sat there watching with tears in my eyes: shocked, saddened, and troubled, feeling extremely guilty and unworthy of all the things I have that I take for granted. I was shocked that so many children die around the world without food every day. ***Food!*** I've always been blessed to have a refrigerator that remains full of food.

I was saddened that many of these precious lives were snuffed out without the opportunity to ever grow old or experience a fraction of the life that I have been so blessed to live. I was troubled about too many of us being so caught up in our own lives that we pretty much remain unaware of the suffering happening all around the world. I felt guilty that I had not done more to help. I hadn't given as much as I could. Finally, I felt extremely unworthy of the many blessings God has blessed me with. I have been extremely fortunate all my life. You have been too.

WINNING THE LOTTERY

I've heard it said that if you are born in America, you have already won the lottery. We have the access to live a life with luxuries that most of the world doesn't even know even exists. When you count the three meals most of us get and two hearty snacks, we get to eat five times a day. That's a blessing considering that as many as 828 million people go to bed hungry every night.[93] That night, at that unlikely time, during halftime of the NBA Finals, I was reminded of how unconcerned and unaware I had been to those who are less fortunate than I am.

Whether we want to admit it or not, humans are born with a natural selfish nature. We think about how things affect us and have a tendency to put ourselves at the center of the universe. It's sad, but true. Think about this current generation of kids

---

93. World Food Programme. "A Global Food Crisis." https://www.wfp.org/global-hunger-crisis.

growing up. They've had a picture taken of themselves pretty much every day of their life. They can order whatever they want and have it delivered to their house the next day. No need to wait until Christmas or a birthday anymore. In his article entitled, "The Most Selfish Generation," Richard K. Vedder says, "Many Americans today, contrary to the path laid out for them by the Greatest Generation, try to maximize their own pleasure and immediate satisfaction at the expense of others."[94] According to a recent study published in the open-access scientific journal *Plos One*, Millennials and Gen Zers are the most self-absorbed generation by far–and by their own admission.[95] Could it be that we are teaching people to be proud of being self-centered and selfish?

You don't have to look too hard to find plenty of examples of negative, selfish behaviors. Selfishness can damage personal relationships, careers, and social connections. We see it play out in every area of life. It seems like the rule to live by in the business world is that you need to do what you need to do in order to get ahead. Malcolm Forbes, businessman born into the wealthy Forbes family, coined the phrase "He who dies with the most toys wins."[96]

Most people in society live by the motto that says life is too short, so do whatever makes you happy. When I was a kid, McDonald's taught me that I deserve a break today. There is so much commercialism all around us, and the goal is to create people who truly believe they are the center of the universe. Mix this with our already strong natural human

---

94. Richard K. Vedder, "The Most Selfish Generation," Independent Institute. https://www.independent.org/news/article.asp?id=14369.
95. *Plos One* journal. https://journals.plos.org/plosone/s/journal-information
96. Wikipedia, "John Malcolm Forbes," https://en.wikipedia.org/wiki/John_Malcolm_Forbes.

tendency to look out for ourselves first while striving to do whatever we must to be on top, and you can see the toxic individualistic worldview permeating our society. Sadly, when a worldview is as deeply rooted in American culture as individualism is, we should not be surprised when it finds its way into the minds of Christians.[97]

THE GOLDEN RULE

This is so contrary to the teachings of Jesus found in the Bible. I remember learning the Golden Rule when I was a kid in vacation Bible school: "Treat each other like you want to be treated; show love and you're going to receive it."[98] Jesus also taught us that the first shall be last and the last first.[99] He modeled servanthood by washing the feet of the disciples and serving them every chance He could. Jesus modeled the philosophy of putting God first, others second, and ourselves last. This is the message of love that embodied His ministry, the one that the disciples finally understood and spread throughout the whole world.

This philosophy is still alive today, although you would be hard pressed to find people who truly practice this, even in the Christian world. Even so, this is the kind of man, the kind of leader, that I'm challenging you to be. Jesus demonstrated that leaders care for people, all people, especially those who are hurting and who are in need.

Near the end of Mark 1, we read about Jesus healing a man who was plagued with leprosy. This was a death sentence that came at the end of a long, painful, lonely illness. The Bible

---

97. Wilkens, Steve and Mark L. Sanford, *Hidden Worldviews: Eight Cultural Stories That Shape Our Lives* (Downers Grove, Ill.: IVP Academic, 2009).
98. Matthew 7:12, NIV.
99. Matthew 19:13, NIV.

says in verse 41 that Jesus was filled with compassion and reached out his hand and touched the man. Jesus didn't have to touch him in order to heal him. He could have just spoken the word and the man would have been instantly healed and cleansed. Yet, Jesus showed compassion and love to a man who most likely hadn't been touched in a long time.

Jesus was the complete opposite of selfish. He was compassionate, loving, and unafraid to be selfless. He taught us that enduring leadership, the kind that makes a positive, long-range difference, is always characterized by compassion.[100] It's so easy for people to say they love others and talk about what they do for other people, but seeing examples of the fruit of real compassion is a little harder to find. I'm encouraging you to be the type of man who is strong enough, secure enough, and established enough that you can make it a priority to help other people.

This concept may be new to you, or you haven't given it much thought. Yet, this has to be more than something you are only reading or thinking about. Concepts like self-sacrifice have to be lived out and exercised on a daily basis. I'm challenging you to rid your mind of selfish thinking and selfish behavior. This type of selfishness has contributed to the problems we are having with men in our society today. Too many of our brothers are looking out for number one first. Too many are chasing their own dreams and abandoning those who depend on them or need them. Too many men are choosing to live "their truth" and not accepting responsibility for their actions or the commitments they have made. Too

---

100. Bob Briner and Ray Pritchard. *Leadership Lessons of Jesus: Timeless Wisdom for Leaders in Today's World* (New York, NY: Random House, 1998).

many men believe that the ends justify the means and they are going to get theirs by any means necessary.

We have bought into the lie that there are only so many pieces of the pie to go around, so it's acceptable to forget about others and go for your own. They are afraid of being left without any of the pie.

LAW OF THE HARVEST

This couldn't be further from the truth and in fact, this type of thinking is completely opposite of what God teaches. A verse I would encourage you to memorize concerning this destructive thinking says, "There is a way that appears to be right, but in the end it leads to death."[101] I have found that when we take the time to invest in the lives of other people, helping them, or doing nice things for them, in return we usually receive a blessing in our lives. We reap what we sow; it's the law of the harvest.[102] If there is one thing I learned from my days working in the cornfields in Illinois detasseling corn, it's the law of the harvest. You always reap what you sow, you reap more than you sow, and you reap after you sow.

This works with positive, good things, but also with negative, bad things. If you want to reap love, kindness, positivity, and goodness, then you have to sow those things. Practice doing nice things for people, showing kindness, being positive and living upright. That's what you will reap. If you want to keep having bad junk happen to you in your life, keep living like a selfish knucklehead.

---
101. Proverbs 14:12, NIV
102. Galatians 6:9, NIV

I look for opportunities to work with people who are doing great things in life and spreading good will towards those around them. I do my best to spend time with people like that because they inspire and challenge me to be more generous and giving. I love having people in my life who are serving others and helping people around them improve their life and accomplish their goals. When I have made attempts to do this on my own and help other people reach their dreams, I usually am blessed more than they are. Many times it's much later, but I have seen how I have benefited from those relationships and have seen countless new opportunities come my way as a result of what I sowed.

God honors this type of attitude and blesses it supernaturally. He likes for us to put others first and consider their needs before our own. He especially likes it and blesses us when we seek to do His will above our own. God's way works. I have seen the fruit of obedience to His ways in my own life in so many ways.

O-LINE IS THE BEST

When I played football in college, I was an offensive lineman. If you've ever watched a football game, you know that not a lot of excitement happens on the offensive line. Everyone wants to watch the highly-paid quarterback or the diva wide receiver. There aren't many people paying attention to what the big, ole offensive linemen are doing, unless one of us gets called for a holding penalty. It goes without saying, people don't cheer for the big hogs or shout their names from the stands. My offensive line coach used to tell me that he and my girlfriend were the only people watching me play, and sometimes even she wouldn't be paying attention to me. Let's be honest, the whole purpose of an offensive lineman is to block and create holes for the running back to run through, pass protect, and give the quarterback time to throw the ball to one of the pretty-boy receivers. I'm not drinking hater-aid!

When the running back gains a lot of yards, very few people notice that this happened because one of the dependable offensive linemen made a good block. At the same time, when the quarterback has enough time in the pocket to complete a pass to the star receiver, after the touchdown celebration, no one shouts the name of the offensive lineman and celebrates his consistent blocking. Nope. In football, a big, talented, good-looking lineman, working hard behind the scenes, makes the skilled players look good. This is teamwork at its best. This is how sports, business, and life in general work. Usually, when the running back looks good and has a phenomenal season, or the quarterback throws for a lot of yards, it is the result of other people helping them look good.

The unselfish attitude of the linemen, with all the players on the team doing their job with a good attitude to the best of their ability, can cultivate a climate of "team first" that others will adopt. Once this happens, the team will work together effectively with a synergy that produces a win. Eventually, at the end of the season, the work of the behind-the-scenes people will get noticed.

Oftentimes, All Conference and All-American awards are handed out. When the skilled players are helped to perform at exceptional levels, they get coaches and scouts to take note of their performance. In the process, these coaches and officials are able to recognize the accomplishments of the others around them as well. This is how I earned All-Conference accolades at the collegiate level. I helped those around me look good by blocking to the best of my ability. Sports solidified the truth of this statement: When I help enough people get what they want–eventually I will get what I want.

PAY IT FORWARD

A few years back, a movie with Helen Hunt, Kevin Spacey, and Haley Joel Osment, was released, called: *"Pay it Forward."* One of the main themes of the movie is that everyone needs to find someone, anyone really, and do something nice for them that is both unexpected and undeserved. Each person does what they can to impact our world, person by person. Before we know it, something big can happen.

Let's strive to live this out tomorrow and each day of our life moving forward. Pick a few people and do something nice and unexpected for them. See what happens when you sow this random act of kindness. I challenge you to join me in this for just one day–and see what can happen. Do something nice to share the love of Christ with another person. Longtime youth pastor Jeanne Mayo calls it being Jesus with skin on.

When you begin to Man UP and help other people get what they want before you think about yourself, I guarantee you will start to notice the difference this will make in your own life. You will see the people around you start to think more positively of you; changing the way they interact with you and treat you. I don't care how big or small your action is, just do something to plant some love and positivity into our world that so desperately needs it. Maybe you'll decide to slip a couple bucks to that homeless person, or open the door for someone. Maybe you'll set aside time to spend with a kid who doesn't have a dad, or maybe you'll invest time in your own family. Just offer love and kindness to someone–anything you can think of.

I'm asking you to Man UP and join me in trying to make a difference in this world–putting our faith into action. Once we have done this, then we will pray that God steps in and accompanies our natural acts of kindness with His supernatural acts that can help put an end to many of our world's problems.

Section 4:
Endurance
Keep Obeying

- **Chapter 14 Positive Thinking**
- **Chapter 15   Learning from Others**
- **Chapter 16   Continuous Improvement**

Chapter 14
Positive Thinking

**Change your thinking
and you can change your attitude.
Change your attitude
and you can change your performance.
Change your performance
and you can change your productivity.
Change your productivity
and you can change your life.**

King David wrote in Psalm 119:105, NLT: "Your word is a lamp for my feet, a light on my path." This advice is not only for his son Solomon, but for all of us who are wise enough to listen. God's Word, the Bible, will show us the way we should go, both day and night. No matter what circumstance you find yourself in, God's Word will lead and guide you in the right direction. This is why it's so important for us to know it. Not just know it, but to obey it. David continually spoke these words to all those under his guidance. He wrote many of the Psalms and inspired many of the Proverbs that were written in the Bible. He understood the power of speaking positive, life-giving, wise words.

The Bible will change your life if you read it and obey it. I'm a living witness of this. I have a practice of reading a portion of Scripture every day and then meditating on it. I've read through the Bible cover to cover about thirty times in six different versions. I learn something new every time. The Bible has truly changed my life.

Knowing God's Word will change your life too. When I worked for well-known Christian author and speaker Joyce Meyer, I remember her saying that studying the Bible is not something we have to do–we study the Bible because we love God, and His Word has the power to change our lives and bring us closer to Him.

THE POWER OF POSITIVE THINKING

I believe in the power of positive thinking. As an adult, I believe I can get more done and will go farther in life if I chose to be a positive person and believe in myself. In his international bestselling book, The Power of Positive Thinking, Norman Vincent Peale said to formulate and stamp in your mind a mental picture of yourself succeeding. He said that whenever a negative thought concerning your personal ability comes to mind, deliberately voice a positive thought to cancel it out. I didn't previously know who Norman Vincent Peale was, but his principle of positive thinking has alway been something I have strived to do.

I was raised in tough circumstances. The only abundance I had growing up was an abundance of love. My family didn't have a lot of money and I didn't always have the nicest things like a lot of other kids. To this day I don't like Michael Jordan because I couldn't afford his shoes when they originally hit the market in the mid-80s. His shoes were mad pricey when they first came out, and even though I knew we couldn't afford them, I badly wanted a pair. Instead, my mom bought me the generic Jordans from K-Mart. I can still hear the kids clownin' me at school when I walked in sporting those kicks. Teenagers can be so cruel.

But, even though the money was always tight, the love I received from my mom and dad was in abundance. This love gave me confidence that would enable me to try new things and eventually succeed at a number of them.

THE KEY TO SUCCESS

Early in life, I bought into the concept of setting goals and working hard in order to accomplish these goals. I was determined to not let my deficient circumstances stop me from soaring to new heights. I admired several people for overcoming challenging upbringings to become successful in their own right. One was Bill Cosby, who started as a comedian, then created the most popular cartoon of my childhood years—Fat Albert. He was successful at stand-up comedy and eventually charged into primetime TV with his number one show—"The Cosby Show." Every black person in America watched that show.

I witnessed the rise in popularity of Oprah Winfrey. She grew up poor, and despite being of average beauty, she landed a job in TV. I remember the first year "The Oprah Winfrey Show" debuted and how I thought it was cool that a black woman had her own show. Now, she's so popular, you don't even have to mention her last name. Everyone knows who you are talking about.

Will Smith is another hard-working brotha who has always intrigued me. I had a boot-leg copy of his cassette, "He's the DJ; I'm the Rapper." I had to keep it hidden because my mom didn't allow me to have secular music in our house growing up. His lyrics were fun and his style was awesome. I was so impressed with this dude. When "The Fresh Prince of Bel-Air" came out, it put Will into the next stratosphere. I was really into music when I was younger and thought to myself that if this young black man from the projects can make it and be successful, then so can I.

These three people have a lot in common, but the one thing that stands out to me most is their positive attitude. I've read their books and seen many interviews in which they expressed that their attitude was a big key to their success. Like all of them, I had to overcome the obstacle of growing up poor. Bill Cosby said, "You can turn painful situations around through laughter. If you can find humor in anything, even poverty, you can survive it."[103] That inspired me to dream outside of living in the projects. Oprah said that when everyone else is feeding themselves on hysteria and negativity, you gotta stay in the light.[104] Will Smith talked about what can happen with positive thinking. He said, "The way you think and what you

---

103. Bill Cosby and Alvin F. Poussaint, *Come on, People: On the Path from Victims to Victors* (Nashville, TN: Thomas Nelson, 2007).
104. YouTube. "Ophrah Winfrey: Motivation to Possess the Power of Positivity," https://www.youtube.com/watch?v=LBAFVYa4eL4.

believe of yourself will have a great impact on your success and your happiness in life."[105]

IT STARTS WITH CHANGE

I'm not saying that I adhere to everything that these three personalities believe or teach, by any means. Each of them is flawed and has made some very public mistakes. However, believing that I can learn from anyone, I took what I needed and developed my own philosophy. Throughout the next few years, on my journey to achieve the goals and dreams I set for myself, I developed the following philosophy:

*Change your thinking
and you can change your attitude,
Change your attitude
and you can change your performance,
Change your performance
and you can change your productivity,
Change your productivity
and you can change your life.*

1) CHANGE YOUR THINKING

It starts with the way you think. You have to learn to control your thinking and channel your thoughts in the right direction. Although this is harder said than done, believe me, it can be done. You have to train yourself how to think. Most people are driven to think by what their emotions tell them. I don't think this is best if you plan to endure the hardships of

---

105. YouTube. "Will Smith on the Power of Positive Thinking." https://www.youtube.com/watch?v=oENmXKKlCAI&t=5s.

life. Here are a few key ways that you need to train yourself to think:

- *Train yourself to think rationally instead of emotionally. Don't let your feelings dictate what you think, which will eventually lead to what you do. In a sermon titled, "Stop Focusing On Negative Emotions," from December 2020, Pastor Steven Furtick said: "Feelings have their place, but it's not on the throne."[106]*
- *Train yourself to think about the long-term consequences of all your thoughts and actions instead of the short-term benefit. Too many people forfeit long-term positive consequences in exchange for a short-term feeling of immediate gratification. We want to feel good now, so we choose not to think about how this decision will affect us later. At other times we may manage to do our due diligence and think things through, but we still end up choosing to go with the short-term benefit. This is wrong too. We will discuss this later when we talk about how our actions need to line up with what we are thinking.*
- *Train yourself to think about positive things versus negative things. Choose to be optimistic versus pessimistic. I know many people who are pessimistic about most things. After a while this pessimism grows into being negative about life in general. They may try to mask their pessimistic and negative attitude by saying they are just a "realist." Same thing! If you are going to be a person who is strong enough to persevere*

---

106. YouTube. "Steven Furtick. Stop Focusing On Negative Emotions," modified December 12, 2020. https://youtu.be/bT1RNuikquo.

through the tough times in life, you are going to have to train yourself to see things in a more positive light. Look at the glass as being half full instead of half empty. Joyce Meyer has a knack for coining phrases that people call "Joyceisms." One of my favorite of her sayings is: "Where the mind goes, the man follows."[107]

Keeping your mind full of positive thoughts is important because you usually see what you think you see. In relationships this is crucially important because without giving people the benefit of the doubt, we will only see them as selfish and untrustworthy. Their flaws will be what we first see, which will lead to a negative perception. We may find ourselves acting cold and keeping our distance from someone because we expect them to treat us rudely. Our perception then becomes our reality. That doesn't mean that our perception is necessarily the truth, but it is the reality we perceive to be true. This is why it's absolutely important to be optimistic about people and make it a practice to give them the benefit of the doubt. Try thinking the best about people until they prove otherwise. Train yourself to not only do this with people, but also with everyday circumstances that life throws your way.

2) YOUR THINKING AFFECTS YOUR ATTITUDE

Thinking is what goes on in our brain; it's the processing part of what we see. Our attitude is the outward display of what we think. Our attitude is what people see; good or bad,

---
107. Joyce Meyer, *Power Thoughts: 12 Strategies to Win the Battle of the Mind* (New York: Thomas Nelson, 2010).

positive or negative. You can generally tell how people think or what they are thinking about by their attitude. It's hard to control your attitude if you can't control your thinking. Many people find their attitude and emotions sporadically run out of control. This is largely because they are not thinking about the right things. No wonder the Bible says in Philippians 4:8 that we should think on things that are *true, noble, right, pure, lovely and admirable.* It tells us to think about things that are *excellent and praiseworthy.* The apostle Pauls gives us this strong advice and we should not quickly dismiss it. Thinking controls attitude which leads to our actions, or as I call it: performance.

3) YOUR ATTITUDE AFFECTS YOUR PERFORMANCE

When I'm talking about performance in this instance, I'm actually speaking of our actions. Our performance is what we are judged on. People notice what you do or how you perform, then treat you accordingly. When I worked in sales, we got paid based on our performance. I repeatedly said this statement to the sales representatives who worked for me. A good deal of focus in a sales environment is placed on performance. Bonuses, raises, promotions, and awards–are all based on people's performance. I saw masses of good sales people fail to perform at high levels on a consistent basis because they could not control their thinking. Their wrong thinking led them to having an attitude that they could not control. This usually hurt their performance. They allowed outside issues to affect their thinking, which ultimately affected their attitude. Their bad attitude or uncontrolled emotions hindered them from focusing. When a salesman doesn't focus in a sales environment, that's usually not a good thing.

4) YOUR PERFORMANCE AFFECTS YOUR PRODUCTIVITY

The way we perform over a period of time indicates how productive we are. All of us are all capable of high achievement and increased productivity. We can all accomplish things that we dream about or imagine, but we first have to conquer the way we think about things. This is why long-term thinking is so important. Realizing high achievement involves a lot of long-term thinking. In addition, we need to control our attitude, and be consistent in our performance over an extended period of time. To see our dreams fulfilled will take time, often many years of thinking and doing the right things.

Many people have accomplished great things in life, much more than they ever thought they could. The sub-four-minute mile, sending a man to the moon, and discovering a cure for disease have all been accomplished because someone thought it could be done. All of these were accomplished as a result of someone changing their thinking about what had been done in the past, and being willing to endure hardship and adversity along the way.

5) YOUR PRODUCTIVITY AFFECTS YOUR LIFE

Changing your life is easy. Changing it for the better is not. We all want to improve our life for the better, but most people aren't willing to adhere to the process and stick with it till the end. Having a better life doesn't just happen overnight. There is no such thing as a magic wand to wave over our heads to suddenly be successful and achieve our goals. Although, if there were such a thing, this brotha would be livin' large. Nevertheless, changing your life is possible, but you have to be committed to growing, not just interested in changing. When you are "interested" in doing something, you only do it when it's convenient, but when you are "committed," you follow through no matter what–no excuses![108] It all starts with making a commitment to change the way you think.

I WANT TO BE LIKE MIKE

While I worked in sales at MCI Worldcom, I hired many people to work for me who were down and almost out in the game of life. Most of them were motivated to do whatever it took to make some money and improve the quality of their life. One young person was a guy that I hired named Mike. He wanted a career change and came to work on my sales team after losing his job as a laborer. Mike's life was a mess. He had recently gone through a divorce and his financial situation was not good. He owed a lot of money to a lot of creditors.

I hired Mike and taught him how to sell, and more importantly, how to think. With all the personal problems he faced at first, Mike found it difficult to control his thinking. Then with all the rejection that came with telemarketing sales, he had a difficult time controlling his attitude as well. I spent time coaching him on sales techniques to overcome objections

---

108. Ken Blanchard, *The Heart of a Leader: Insights on the Art of Influence.* (Escondido, CA: Honor Books, 1999).

and even more, I spent time addressing his thought process. Mike started listening and eventually started changing his thinking. He made a decision to come into work every day with a positive attitude, regardless of the craziness in life. He realized that he could not allow his circumstances to negatively affect him. He soon became known around the business as being a positive person.

Along with his renewed positive attitude, Mike learned an effective approach to addressing the resistance and fighting through the constant phone rejections. He quickly became a top performer and was recognized for his top productivity at several award ceremonies. He eventually met a girl and became financially secure enough to ask her to marry him. She said yes and they started their own blended family together. His life was back on track and it all started with his thinking. Changing his life wasn't easy, but his hard work and determination made it possible.

LEARNING TO THINK LIKE GOD

I believe all of us are capable of high achievement. We can all accomplish things that we dream about or imagine, but we first have to conquer the way we think about these things. Additionally, I personally believe that in order to achieve all that we are destined to achieve in this life, it requires us to think on a higher, more divine level. God has given us all a purpose in life and He wants us all to accomplish certain things. In order to fulfill this purpose, we have to change our thinking to be more in line with His thinking.

In Ezekiel 11:19, God says that He will give us a desire to respect Him completely, He will put inside us a new way of thinking. He says He will remove our stubborn heart that is focused on ourselves, what we want, and think we need–He calls this a heart of stone. God goes on to say that He will then teach us how to think. We will learn to think about obeying Him and His laws and decrees–He calls this having a heart of flesh. The next verse says that once we learn how to think, then we will start to live by God's rules and obey His laws. That's when we will be known as His people, the people of God.[109]

Wow, what a promise! We don't even have to do it all by ourselves. God will help us if we ask Him to.

Norman Vincent Peale encouraged us to try what he called Prayer Power. In his book, *The Power of Positive Thinking* (which if you have not read, you definitely need to), Peale tells the story of two men having a serious conversation. One of them was troubled by a business and personal crisis. He went to his coworker, who was considered a man of great wisdom and understanding, for advice. Together they both explored the problem from every angle but seemingly without result, which only deepened the troubled man's discouragement. He concluded that there was no power on earth that could save him. The wise man of understanding thought for a moment, then said, "I believe you are wrong in saying there is no power that can save you. I have found there is a solution to every problem. There is a power that can help you. Why not try prayer power?"[110]

109. Ezekiel 11:19–20, NIV.
110. Norman Vincent Peale, *The Power of Positive Thinking* (New York: Simon and Schuster, 2008 edition).

The way to Man UP and change your thinking is to allow God to help you. He will teach you and direct you, but you have to humble yourself and ask Him. Then be prepared to obey what He tells you–and keep obeying. He has a good plan for you, "to prosper you and not to harm you, plans to give you hope and a future" (Jeremiah 29:11, NIV).

Chapter 15
Learning from Others

If there would be one issue I have with King David, it's that he didn't appear to be the best father. His family was filled with so much drama after his wicked sin with Bathsheba. David may have believed he had gotten away with minimal consequences to his sin. Thus far, as prophesied by the prophet Nathan, the child born from David's adultery died. God was displeased with David, but because of his repentant heart, He did not kill him. Yet, Nathan informed King David that the consequence of his sin would be that the sword would never depart from his house. God's plan was to bring calamity and tragedy on David's family all the remaining days of his life.[111] Brought on by his own sinful behavior and his failure as a father, David sat by and idly watched as his kids–as the old heads would say–ran around acting foolishly.

---
111. 2 Samuel 12:7–13, NIV.

The first incident occurred between David's son Amnon and his half-sister Tamar, a very beautiful woman. Just as David lusted after Bathsheba, Amnon had some of the same weaknesses as his father David. He tried to seduce her, but when she refused his advances, he raped her. After the dreadful act had been committed, however, his desire for her was turned to hatred. He drove her away in his fury.[112] To make matters worse, when David found out about this, he did nothing.

This ordeal led to a second messed-up situation in David's family. When Tamar's brother, Absalom, realized what had happened, and that their father, David, did nothing to address the situation, he was outraged. Absalom didn't say a word about the incident to Amnon for two long years, but he devised a plan to take revenge on his half brother. The opportunity finally arrived. Absalom needed to visit sheep shearers in Baal-hazor, so he invited his brothers to go with him. While they were there, Absalom got Amnon drunk and then had his men kill him. He took matters in his own hands to avenge his sister's rape since their father didn't address it.

This story is a reminder that problems don't go away on their own; they need to be dealt with. It's important to know God's Word, so we can have wisdom to navigate the difficult situations in life.

That's not the end of David's family drama. So far he had one son who raped his sister, and another son who killed the brother who committed the rape. Now, David had to deal with Absalom's actions. Again, he decided to do nothing except send him away into exile and not speak to him. This went on

---

112. 2 Samuel 13:3–19, NIV.

for three years, but David missed his son and wanted to see him again.

Meanwhile, Joab, David's nephew and the commander of Israel's army, conspired with his cousin Absalom to help bring him back from exile. Absalom began to work behind the king's back to curry favor with the people of Israel. He finally gathered enough support that he felt he was ready to take the throne from David by force. David was totally unaware of the growing rebellion. He was occupied gathering materials for the Temple that would eventually be built by the next generation on his throne, his son Solomon. When he finally learned of the uprising, he felt that the forces of Absalom had become too strong so he took an entourage and fled his capital, Jerusalem. While David left the capital city, Absalom publicly slept with his father's concubines to further show his strength.

Ultimately, Absalom's rebellion didn't work and he ended up being captured when his hair got stuck in a tree. Even though David gave explicit orders that Absalom was to be captured alive, Joab killed Absalom while he was suspended in the tree.[113] The emotional drain of these tragic events left David tired, weak, and broken. Never would the king be the same; never would his kingdom be the same either.

You would think all of this would have motivated David to finally get his house in order. Sadly, it didn't. Old age was upon him and when the time drew near for someone to replace him as king, he was once again silent. Apparently he had made private assurances to Bathsheba that her son

---

113. 2 Samuel 15 and 16, NIV.

Solomon would sit on the throne when he died.[114] However, Adonijah, David's oldest living son, believing he was next in line began to take steps to achieve recognition as Israel's next king. He lined up his supporters and threw a banquet to celebrate his own coronation.

However, at the same time, in a small quiet coronation that included Zadok the priest, and Israel's prophet Nathan, David made it official by passing along the crown to Solomon. Word quickly spread to the people, and they began to shout that King David had made Solomon the next king. All this happened without David focusing on peace and unity in his own family by having a conversation with his children to explain his succession plan. Nope! Adonijah, feeling slighted, tried to devise a subtle plan to steal the throne from his brother Solomon. This stuff would make a great movie, wouldn't it? Solomon recognized Adonijah's trickery and had him put to death.

The latter years of David's life were not the best. To say the least, they were tragic. It remains to be said that David wasn't the best father. He lived to see three of his sons die, and another was killed shortly after his death, his daughter was raped by her brother, and the entire city watched his own son, Absalom, openly embarrass him by sleeping with his concubines. Talk about family drama!

In spite of all of David's problems with his children, we can still see the faithfulness of God to him. The Lord never left David or forsook him. He provided the grace to live through every situation. David was great in his sin, but he was also great in his repentance. That same provision is still available

---

114. 1 Kings 1:15–21, NIV.

today to every child of God, no matter what situation we are in. We learn a valuable lesson that can save us a lot of heartache in our own personal life just by avoiding David's missteps.[115] When we are strong, and learn the Lord's commands, obey them and keep obeying them, we will live a prosperous life.

AVERAGE, WISE, OR FOOLISH

I've come to live by a motto that was adopted from a quote believed to come from German statesman and diplomat, Otto von Bismarck. He said, "Only a fool learns from his own mistakes. The wise man learns from the mistakes of others."[116] I don't know if I originally heard this phrase wrong, but somewhere along the line I changed it.

I grew up without much contact with my real dad because he was in and out of prison most of my formative years. I really don't know how many times he has been locked up or for how long in total, I just know that he hasn't been around for much of my life. I would be lying if I said that it didn't bother me. I'm a fifty-year-old father of five who has a great life and a wonderful relationship with all of my kids. I have had the privilege of raising all of them in the home with their mother, whom I have been married to for twenty-seven years. I'm a blessed man. I've been motivated to Man UP and raise my own kids, largely because I didn't want my kids to experience the hurt that I carry.

Although I didn't have much contact with my real dad, I always knew what was going on with him and I endeavored to not repeat the same mistakes he made. He dropped

---

115. Fred Hartman, "David And His Children–Tragedy!," *Israel My Glory,* June/July 1986. https://israelmyglory.org/article/david-and-his-children-tragedy/.
116. A to Z Quotes. Otto von Bismarck. https://www.azquotes.com/quote/419698

out of high school, so I strive to get as much education as I can. He started using drugs at a young age, so I've never touched drugs. He has several different kids by a few different women, so I decided to lock my family up and keep it in my pants until I was married and ready to have kids. He ended up locked up, and since I'm too pretty for jail, I do my best to stay out of trouble.

However, I have been in jail many times in a few different states and several countries. I have had the honor of doing jail ministry all around the world, including Venezuela, Albania, Dominican Republic, South Africa, and the U.S.

Whenever I walk into a jail and talk with the inmates imprisoned there, I share my story of what it's like growing up without a dad. Then I tell them of the successful life that I live now and leave them with this statement: "The average person learns from their own mistakes, the wise person from the mistakes of others, but a fool never learns." Then I boldly, and if I weren't as big as I am, possibly a little foolishly, point out that since they are sitting in jail–they are already proven to be fools, or at best average. I then challenge them to decide to change ways. I tell them it starts with their thinking, then their attitude, then their performance, then they can change their life. I'm determined to learn from the mistakes of others and use that as fuel to help other people.

DENISE'S STORY

Early on in our marriage, my wife and I had one of our friends live with us for a while. Her name was Denise. She was a recovering drug user that I developed a unique friendship with. We had many long talks about life, God, friendship, family, you name it. When I met Denise she had committed her heart to God and was on the road to recovery. She was in a residential drug treatment program called Teen Challenge, although she was well out of her teen years. Teen Challenge is committed to helping men and women of all ages reclaim their lives from the addictions of drugs and other substances. Denise's goal at this time was to get well enough to get her life back on track. She wanted to find a job and prove herself stable enough to have her teenage daughter come live with her again.

Because of her history of drug abuse, Denise lost everything near and dear to her. She lost her job as a nurse. She ostracized herself from her family because she constantly stole from them to buy drugs. Sadly, Denise proved that she was incapable of taking care of her daughter because she wasn't in control of her life–drugs were. So she lost custody of her daughter who ended up being raised by Denise's sister.

At the point we became friends, things were changing for Denise. She was about ready to finish her time in the Teen Challenge program and needed a place to go for a fresh start. She knew she couldn't return to her hometown because too many triggers would tempt her to return to her old lifestyle. If she were to remain clean, she knew she couldn't reenter the same old life, full of the same old friends, offering her the same old drugs, to escape the same old worries of life.

DENISE LESSON #1–REMEMBER THE GOLDEN RULE

At the time, my wife was the program director for the Teen Challenge Denise was in. Ang is a great Christian lady who really takes the Golden Rule to heart. The Golden Rule says:

"This is how we know what real love is: Jesus gave his life for us. So we should give our lives for our brothers and sisters. Suppose someone has enough to live and sees a brother or sister in need, but does not help. Then God's love is not living in that person. My children, we should love people not only with words and talk, but by our actions and true caring" (1 John 3:16–18, NIV).

I was taught the Golden Rule as a child and I did my best to live by it. Jesus wants us to be nice and kind to other people. Got it! But I thought I only had limited responsibility to be polite to people in social settings, like at grocery stores or restaurants. My understanding of the Golden Rule is that it requires limited acts of service from me. Little things like offering my chair to elderly people or women when needed; that I should not have road rage and that I should willingly let other people cut in my lane of traffic. I thought my responsibility ended once I offered a nice and polite gesture to show that I was a friendly neighbor. You know, little stuff like that.

However, no one ever said the Golden Rule would include letting a recovering drug dealer move into my small two-bedroom apartment with me and my newlywed wife. Never would I have thought this was a part of the Golden Rule.

Whelp. You guessed it! Angie extended the invitation for Denise to live with us, for free nonetheless. So for the next seven months we had a new roommate. Even though we had our share of small inconveniences, we helped Denise get back on her feet. We helped her get a well-paying job and a car so that she could get around on her own. She was doing great.

I vividly remember a deep discussion we had when Denise opened up about her past. I asked her to explain how she had arrived the point she was at in her life. She began by telling me she never thought she would be where she was now. She had hit rock bottom. She reminisced back to the days when she was a nurse in Buffalo, New York. She blew that job by stealing narcotics from the hospital in order to get high. She told me about growing up and experimenting with marijuana in her early teen years. She told me about how she would steal from anyone and everyone, including her family, to get high. I asked her how she got started and she told me her *friends* introduced her to drugs. Did you catch that?

DENISE LESSON #2–SHOW ME YOUR FRIENDS AND I'LL SHOW YOU YOUR FUTURE

I want to be clear, Denise did not blame her drug use, or any of the tough times she experienced in life, on her friends. She admitted she was the one who made the choice to do drugs the first time. No one was to blame except herself. However, it is fair to point out that she was introduced to drugs the first time by her friends. They influenced her in a negative way by pressuring her to try drugs. This initial experiment would turn into habitual use and then sadly, drugs would define who she was for the rest of her life.

Wisdom reveals that you need to choose your friends wisely. They will encourage you to either do great things or destructive things. Realize that none of us are above being influenced. It's imperative that you choose to be influenced by people who are positive, honorable, and respectful of others.

Surround yourself with good people. Legendary business tycoon Andrew Carnegie said, "Never be so foolish as not to surround yourself with people who are smarter than you."

King David gave this advice to Solomon as he gave him final instructions as his administration ended and Solomon's was beginning. In particular, David gave Solomon advice on how to deal with the wicked commander of his army, Joab. David told Solomon to completely eliminate Joab from his administration. Even though Joab had led the army in many victories for many years, David knew that he was not a good person for Solomon to keep around. He advised his son to choose wisely which men he would give power and authority to. This was one of the first difficult decisions Solomon would have to Man UP and make.

BEING COOL ISN'T WORTH IT

When I was a youth pastor, I told young people all the time to make sure they chose their friends wisely. I saw herds of young people make poor choices that negatively directed the course of their lives forever–all because they allowed their friends to influence them in destructive ways. They wanted to be cool so they tried drugs for the first time, and ten years later, they were still addicted. They wanted to fit in so they started to go to the wild parties and ended up getting drunk for the first time. They got caught driving drunk while under age. Ten years later, they were working through the ramifications of having their third DUI, and to this day, still aren't able to drive legally.

I saw people who wanted to be in relationships so desperately that they started dating too soon. They got involved in a bad relationship with the wrong person who was way too old for them and didn't have their values. Ten years later they found themselves still unmarried, but living on welfare in the projects trying to raise three little kids on their own. All of these lives were negatively affected because people chose to spend time with, and be influenced by, the wrong people. Learn to learn from others.

WHAT ABOUT DENISE?

I didn't finish the story of Denise. Like I said, she did pretty well for a while. She allowed my wife and a couple of other Christian women to influence her and help lead her life in the right direction. She appeared to be on the right track and was even able to have her daughter come live with her again. Then things took a turn for the worse.

Denise was clean and sober for a couple of years, but then she got hooked back up with the wrong crowd. She started hanging around people who smoked cigarettes. Although she tried to hide it, before long before she started smoking again too. It didn't take long before smoking cigarettes turned into smoking pot, then the other drugs quickly followed. Denise was back on drugs and then she disappeared. We didn't hear from her for about five years. Every now and then we would receive reports of her life and how she would move around from place to place looking for the next high.

Then one day we received a phone call from a friend who told us Denise was in the hospital. She was fighting for her life. It was like a scene right out of the movies. My wife and I arrived at the hospital to find she was in a coma. Her new friends, the ones she was abusing drugs with, realized she had overdosed. They drove her to the hospital and dropped her off at the door and drove off so they wouldn't get caught using illegal drugs.

She was only in the hospital for a week or so. The doctors did everything they could to help her recover, but her body couldn't handle all the years of abusing drugs. She died. Cause of death: years of poor influence from "so called" friends. I spoke at her funeral.

Who you truly are is seen in your actions. Denise's life didn't have to end this way. Sure, she made some poor choices. She abused drugs for a long time. It all started by her choosing to follow the wrong crowd. Learn from the mistakes of my friend Denise and choose your friends wisely. Surround yourself with friends who will encourage you to be a better person and to strive to live a good, honorable, God-pleasing life. God used Denise to reinforce two valuable lessons in my life:

1. *The Golden Rule–Treat other people like you want to be treated.*
2. *Choose your friends wisely.*

I share the story of my friend Denise to honor her life. If only one person learns from her mistakes, it would be worth it. I pray that you Man UP and learn these life lessons too. Walk in the way of the Lord and be blessed. Real men are determined to journey through life by living in obedience to God's Word. They are determined to follow other wise people that they can learn from. I've learned that you can't follow the crowd and Man UP at the same time.

Chapter 16
Continuous Improvement

"When you stop learning, you stop growing." Albert Einstein said that, and it's always fascinated me. When we cease to learn, we cease to grow. And when we cease to grow, we cease to improve, get better, move forward, and just sort of–exist.[117] Deep down, I believe everyone wants to become the best person they can be, but in order for this to happen, you have to constantly and continually work at getting better. Becoming a better you is about always improving who you are as a person. It takes continually striving to reach your full potential and a lasting commitment to constantly grow and mature. This applies to every area of your life–your thinking, your feelings, and your actions. We have to be committed to continual improvement.

---

117. Robert Kiyosaki, Facebook post, August 25, 2017.

I was originally introduced to the concept of continual improvement while in college at Evangel University. One of my business professors taught about the life and work of Edwards Deming. Dr. Deming is known as the father of the Japanese post-war industrial revival. Before that, he was regarded by many as a quality guru in the United States. His expertise was used by the United States during World War II in an effort to help improve the quality of war materials. His background was in mathematics and statistics, but many in the U.S. initially didn't regard his philosophies very highly. After the war, when the Japanese industrial leaders invited him to Japan to help improve the quality of their industrial products, he quickly took this opportunity.

In only four short years, the world began to see that Japan—which immediately after the war was perceived as producing cheap quality goods—was now producing quality products. Dr. Deming was invited back to Japan year after year and the Japanese scientists and engineers named an award after him, honoring organizations that achieve high quality-performance criteria. Deming summarized his business philosophy in a work known as Deming's Fourteen Points. These points set the tone for a lot of U.S. companies and challenged them to strive for increased quality control that would result in continuous improvement.[118]

My professor taught the fourteen points, along with other Deming concepts like Total Quality Management, and, of course, continuous improvement, which is woven all throughout the Fourteen Points. It's mentioned again and again in

---

118. Class notes from business class at Evangel University, 1993. Also, Wikipedia. https://en.wikipedia.org/wiki/W._Edwards_Deming, accessed April 1, 2023.

several of the points. This concept immediately made sense to me and I was totally on board. I was reminded of what my dad and uncle Ronnie taught about always striving to get better at everything I do. In sports, it didn't matter if I was on the football field or throwing the discus in a track competition, I always wanted to be better than before. My goal was to improve each and every time I did something.

Now that I was formally studying the practical points in my business class, I knew right away I was being given an accelerator that others didn't have. I was determined to pay close attention and really learn these concepts so that I would be set up for success in every area of life.

TOTAL QUALITY MANAGEMENT

I've had careers in the business world and in church ministry and these points have helped me be an effective leader in both areas. In life, business, or ministry, I believe we should always continually strive to improve. When adopted and applied, Deming's points will help bring systems and process to your life. People don't often think about how valuable organization and production skills are. They go a long way to ensuring long-term initiatives and goals are met. Adherence to systems produces endurance. I won't go into all fourteen of the points, although it would be worth your own research at some point. Here are a few of the main points that I have applied in my life, business, and ministry:

- **Improve every process.** *Always examine your systems and processes to identify problems in order to*

improve every activity you do. This ensures what you produce is always improving in quality and service.
- **Create constancy of purpose.** *This is using innovation effectively and ensuring the allocation of resources to improve your products or services. Start thinking about long-term needs rather than short-term profitability in order to stay competitive in your field.*
- **Pride of workmanship.** *Always work to produce a quality product and insist everyone on your team does the same.*
- **Encourage education.** *Create a culture that encourages self improvement for everyone. This point has helped me personally more than any of the others. I consistently read three books every month and I've continued working towards my formal education, having recently earned my master's degree and currently working towards my doctoral degree.*
- **Work as a team.** *Break down barriers between departments and staff areas. People in different areas must work in teams to tackle problems.*
- **Institute leadership.** *Focus on becoming a leader who helps others do a better job. The responsibility of a leader must be changed from focusing on numbers to ensuring high quality work is being done all throughout the organization. Improvement of quality will automatically improve productivity.*[119]

---

119. The Deming Institute. "Fourteen Points," https://deming.org/explore/fourteen-points/.

Continuous Improvement

The goal is to get a little better all the time. To always strive to improve in our performance and in our life. No matter who you are in life or what you do, you have to strive to get better. This is the way God intended for us. We were created to always grow and mature, but how fast we grow or how much we mature is up to us.

TEAM DYNASTIES

Look at this in other areas of life. Because of my love of sports, I will go back to the sports examples. Regardless of the sport, it's rare to see a team win a championship year after year. With very few exceptions, in any of the major sports (football, baseball, basketball), at any level, either college or pro, it's hard to find a team dynasty. I would describe a dynasty as a team that wins multiple championships for an extended length of time like ten to fifteen years.

In recent years, teams have at times won championships back to back, possibly even three in a row, or even three out of four years in a row. In my lifetime, I think about the 1990s Chicago Bulls, who won six championships in eight years, with two sets of three consecutive championships. I would even give props to the early 2000s Los Angeles Lakers. Led by my guy Shaquille O'Neal, in five seasons, the Lakers won four Western Conference titles in 2000, 2001, 2002 and 2004, accomplishing a three-peat in the process by winning championships from 2000 to 2002.[120] I'll even show some love to the Alabama Crimson Tide. Coach Nick Saban has won six National Championships in the past twelve college football

---

120. "Dynasty (sports)," https://en.wikipedia.org/wiki/Dynasty_(sports).

seasons. He's also had three national runner-up finishes during that time. Roll Tide.[121]

And, of course, I should mention the New England Patriots, led by Brady and Belichick, who won six Super Bowl titles in nineteen years from 2001–2019. During that run they won three Super Bowls in four years, and had three other Super Bowl appearances. Brady played in nine Super Bowls during that span. That's impressive.

There have been a lot of impressive teams in history and I imagine right now you are upset that I didn't mention your favorite team. Simma down, now! If I didn't include the greatest team of all time–my beloved '85 Bears, I'm not about to mention your junkie team. Nonetheless, you don't see many teams anymore like the UCLA Bruins or Boston Celtics who won ten and eleven championships during their dynasties. (*Side note:* in doing my research, I found that the Green Bay Packers of old won a lot of championships in the 40s and 50s. However, as a die hard Bears fan, I just couldn't bring myself to give them any love in my book. I just couldn't do it!)

The UCLA Bruins men's basketball team from 1964 to 1975, under John Wooden, won ten national championships in twelve seasons. They included a streak of seven consecutive championships from 1967 to 1973, four undefeated seasons, and an NCAA record eighty-eight consecutive wins.[122] Perhaps even more impressive, in twenty seasons, the Boston Celtics won thirteen NBA championships. They won an unprecedented eight consecutive championships during

---

121. "Dynasty (sports)," https://en.wikipedia.org/wiki/Dynasty_(sports)#cite_note-160.
122. Puma, Mike. "Sportscenter Biography: Wizard of Westwood". ESPN Classic. From February 8, 2010.

that run and played in ten straight NBA finals. I don't believe we will ever see dominance like that again in the NBA.[123]

Although, while researching for this book, I was shocked to discover the dominance of the University of Connecticut women's basketball team. Under Geno Auriemma from 1995 through 2022, they won eleven championships in seventeen seasons, including three consecutive championships from 2002 to 2004 and four consecutive from 2013 to 2016. During that run, they've had five undefeated seasons in 2002, 2009, 2010, 2014 and 2016.[124] Coach Geno, just so you know: my daughter is already six foot tall and she's only thirteen years old. She's a beast on her seventh grade girls basketball team. Hit a brotha up.

We could debate about many other great teams—whether they were truly a dynasty or not. It's fun to hear the sports reporters debate this topic on ESPN. It causes me to question, however, why we don't see more dynasties these days. I surmise that with increased competition and decreased player loyalty, it's harder for teams to continually improve year after year like they did in the past.

When a team starts to show signs of dominance today, other teams grow tired of losing and do whatever it takes to recruit more talented players so they can take down the champs. Oftentimes, the winning teams lose quality players to other teams that are willing to pay them more money. For whatever reasons, once a team gets to the top, they tend to be satisfied with their past success instead of working even harder to

---

123. *Sports Illustrated*. March 6, 1999, "SI's Top 20 Dynasties of the 20th Century."
124. *Chicago Tribune*. April 1, 2016. "UConn women may be the greatest college basketball dynasty ever."

improve. Teams that fail to improve can't expect to keep on winning in an ever increased competitive world.

NATURAL TALENT AND ABILITY ONLY TAKE US SO FAR

The same is true of us. Many of us are born with natural talent and ability that God has blessed us with. God gives us these talents and abilities generously according to the purpose He has for us to fulfill in life. Think about this for a moment. Have you ever met someone you thought was good at everything? I mean they are good looking, good athletes, musically inclined, very smart, have great people skills, and everyone just seems to love them. Back in the day we would say, "They got it going on." Those are the kind of people you love to hate, but you actually like them because they are really nice too. Do you know anyone like that? Some of you are going way back, possibly even to high school or junior high, to think of that guy.

When you think about all the natural talent and ability that person had, unless they are committed to continually working to improve, they will be just another average guy in a few years. Whatever happened to "Mr. or Mrs. Most Likely to Succeed" in your high school graduating class? Did they? It's sad to see people who appeared to have it all together and talented now working at the local grocery store while still living at home with their parents. After graduation, they didn't grow. They weren't committed to continually improving. They got stuck.

All of us have to continue to improve in life. Natural talent and ability can only go so far. Beauty fades, fortunes are spent, and skills diminish. Awareness requires that we work to always improve ourselves. Jesus himself modeled this for us. From the time He came to earth, He was committed to growth. The Bible says in Luke 2:52, "Jesus increased in wisdom and in stature and in favor with God and man." I want that to be said of me; that Alex always increased in wisdom and in stature and he had favor with God and people.

PERFECT PRACTICE MAKES PERFECT

The more you do something, the better at it you get. Therefore, don't just practice, but take the time to practice doing things the right way. Nolan Richardson, head men's basketball coach of the Arkansas Razorbacks, led the team to a national championship in 1994, and to the finals in 1995, only to lose to UCLA. He shared this concept at a leadership conference where he was the keynote speaker. He challenged and inspired all of us when he shared his philosophy of getting a little better every day. His championship team didn't just practice each day, but they focused on practicing doing things the right way.

We see an obvious difference between great performers and good performers. The difference comes in the amount of time the great performers are willing to spend on the practice field. The greatest receiver to ever play in the NFL, without a doubt, is Jerry Rice. He was known for being the first player on the practice field and the last one to leave. He practiced running his pass routes to perfection well after the regular practice ended. Many times, other players saw him running passing routes by himself with no one left to throw the ball to him. That's an awful lot of running to do, to not even catch the ball.

He wasn't the fastest or the biggest, but he had the best work ethic—and he knew the secret was to practice perfection. It paid off for him.

Dan Marino and John Elway are two of the greatest quarterbacks to ever play the game. They were known for throwing so many passes during practice that their arms would hurt and they would have to ice them. Neither of these guys were born with the most natural talent and ability. Yet they began with what they had to work with and added a lot of effort and commitment to practice perfection. It paid off for them too.

Tiger Woods started practicing the game of golf when he was three years old. By the time Tiger was a teenager, he was better than a lot of the professionals on tour. His dad insisted he spend countless hours every day, practicing all the intricacies of the game of golf—his swing, reading greens, putting, chipping, and more. Tiger spent hours upon hours practicing hitting the ball perfectly in his quest to be the greatest golfer of all time.[125] The result? Tiger was dominant during his career. He has eighty-two all-time PGA tour victories (tied with Sam Snead for the most of all time). He won eighteen Majors. He's one of only five players to achieve the career Grand Slam, the youngest to do so. He's only the second golfer out of two (after Nicklaus) to achieve a career Grand Slam three times.[126] The hours of perfect practice on the golf course paid off for him too.

These people were willing to put in the time and practice their skill, their talent, their art, until they perfected it. That's what it takes to be great.

---

125. Jeff Benedict and Armen Keteyian, *Tiger Woods* (New York: Simon and Schuster, 2018).
126. Tiger Woods. "Biography," https://tigerwoods.com

REPETITION IS THE KEY TO LEARNING

Today, people don't like to practice. I can still hear Allen Iverson giving the iconic "practice" rant in a press conference after a tough loss. "We sitting here talking about practice. Not a game. Practice. I'm supposed to be the franchise player and we talking about practice! Practice man. Not a game. Practice!"[127] He obviously didn't see the value of practice.

I find this to be the case especially with the younger generation. However, the crazy thing is they are the first ones to say how great they want to be. Some players have this mindset and belief that they are born winners and born to be great. They think it will just happen for them. I find it ironic that even though he was extremely talented and gifted, Allen Iverson never won a championship.

Being great takes a strong commitment to doing what it takes to improve every day–to endure. Since natural talent and ability will only get you so far in life, where your talent leaves off, perfect practice has to begin.

The people who actually become great in life have the discipline, the will power, and the determination to make themselves practice. And practice they do; over and over and over again. They have realized that repetition is the key to learning. I'll say it again, *repetition is the key to learning*. I had to repeat myself so that you were sure to catch it.

Repetition has to assist your discipline, will power, and determination. Practice doing things right and practice doing them over and over and you will certainly become great at it.

---

127. Allen Iverson "Practice" Rant. May 7, 2002. https://www.youtube.com/watch?v=tknXRyUEJtU.

WELL-ROUNDED LEADERS

We should seek to improve ourselves, in every area of our lives, for the rest of our lives. That's the heart of the message of Edwards Demings continuous improvement philosophy. It's not easy and it will require a lot of hard work, but it will be worth it in the end. In your *intellectual* capacity, continue to educate yourself and feed your mind. Set a yearly reading goal, attend conferences and lectures, or even consider continuing your formal education. *Socially,* you should always work to expand your network of friends and acquaintances. Strive to spend time with people who add value to your life. *Mentally*, keep examining yourself to ensure you are not allowing past hurts to resurface and derail your mental growth. Find a wise older mentor or speak with a counselor to help you process difficult things in life. *Physically*, keep a normal exercise routine and maintain a healthy diet. *Spiritually* we should always work to ensure that our relationship with God is growing and maturing every day. Make sure you seek God first, above anything else. He promises that when you seek His Kingdom above all else, and live righteously, He will give you everything you need.[128]

In every area of our lives we have to work at improving all the time. There is no standing still or maintaining; either we are improving or we are declining.

Unfortunately, too many men are revealing they are not willing to give the time and effort to be great. Too many of our brothers are dropping the ball with their responsibilities to their family, their church, and their community. Too many men are not excelling in their vocational calling as

---

128. Matthew 6:33, NLT.

well. Instead of seeking a career they can be proud of, that brings them fulfillment, and provides for their family, they are settling for jobs that barely pay the bills. This is not what God has in store for you, my brotha. It takes a lot of focused energy, effort, time, and even practice to be good enough at any particular skill to be considered a professional. Being considered a professional means you are one of the best at performing that skill or in that area. I have seen many people miss out on greatness because they confused being efficient with cutting corners. To become a professional, one of the best in the game, you have to practice doing things the right way all the time.

WORKING FOR KINGS

The mental preparation is usually missing. The first step is mentally deciding we will give what it takes in order to be great. Think it through and count the costs. It won't necessarily be easy and most of the time, your flesh isn't going to want to pay the price. That's because once we make the decision to do what it takes, we know we are going to have to follow through.

When it comes to taking action, that's where a lot of people are lost. For some, doing what it takes is not natural. For some, it doesn't come easily. For others, it takes a long time dealing with a lot of failed attempts and as a result, people give up too soon; just before they reach greatness. My old football coach used to say that the only place success comes before work is in the dictionary. I've used that hundreds of times, Coach Linn. You'd be proud.

Still others drop out shortly after beginning to take action. They have good intentions but no follow through. I have heard it said that the road to hell is paved with good intentions. I would also say the road to failure is paved with good intentions.

Finally, some people take action and practice over and over; however, they do not practice doing things the right way. These people burn out before they reach their goal because they are not receiving the expected results.

This is why training is so important. Paying attention and learning what to do is extremely important. One of the reasons Solomon was considered one of the best kings of Israel is because he paid attention to what was expected of him before he took the job. He witnessed the good, the bad, and the ugly from his father's administration. He made sure that before he began his administration, he knew what to do. Then he passed along this wisdom to any who would listen when he recorded it in one of the books he wrote. Proverbs 22:29, NLT: "Do you see any truly competent workers? They will serve kings rather than working for ordinary people."[129]

Hear me when I say this. I believe you can excel at just about anything you want to do with enough time, effort, and practice. Sadly, even with this knowledge, most people aren't willing to spend time practicing.

In his 2008 book *Outliers*, Malcolm Gladwell wrote that "10,000 hours is the magic number of greatness." The meaning behind this, in theory, is simple. To be considered elite and truly experienced within a certain craft, you must practice it for ten thousand hours. As Gladwell tells it, the rule

---

129. Proverbs 22:29, NLT.

goes like this: it takes 10,000 hours of intensive practice to achieve mastery of complex skills and materials, like playing the violin or getting as good as Bill Gates at computer programming.[130] Think about it. When you find a career you enjoy that brings you fulfillment, you can become an expert in less than five short years. All you have to do is work diligently and be committed to continually improving every day for forty hours a week. You can do that. Let's go!

WHAT'S STOPPING YOU?

People today have too many interests and are pulled in so many different directions that it's hard for them to stay focused. In the past, people had fewer options so they could focus more easily. They had fewer distractions and less options to vie for their time and attention. Now, the choices are endless and the options are varied. People can be involved with and try so many different things that it becomes counterproductive. They spend a lot of time doing a little of everything and miss out on the opportunity to become an expert or professional at one thing.

Life naturally moves forward. If we sit still, we will lose ground. We have to train ourselves to think of continuous improvement. It's kind of like a car on a hill, it is either being driven forward uphill or it will roll backwards. We can't sit still and stay where we have always been with our talents, skills, ability, and intellectual capacity, or we will naturally fall backwards. The point is simply that cultivating natural

---

130. Malcolm Gladwell, *Outliers: The Story of Success* (New York: Little, Brown and Company, 2008).

ability requires a huge investment of time in order to be clearly seen.

THE ESSENCE OF SURVIVAL

For the past fifteen years, I have had a motivation picture with a quote sitting on my desk. It is the picture of a lion staring dead into the camera with a fable written by Abe Gubegna, Ethiopian novelist and playwright. Although it's not clear if this was the original title, it's become known as, "The Essence of Survival." It says:

> *Every morning in Africa, a gazelle wakes up.*
> *It knows it must run faster than the fastest lion*
> *or it will be killed.*
> *Every morning a lion wakes up.*
> *It knows it must outrun the slowest gazelle*
> *or it will starve to death.*
> *It doesn't matter whether you are a lion*
> *or a gazelle.*
> *When the sun comes up,*
> *you'd better be running.*

Continuous improvement is about waking up every day and realizing you must start the race better than you were the day before. It is a decision you make every day, to wake up and decide you are going to start running. You have to think about how you can improve and then do what it takes to improve. That's what Manning UP is all about.

Section 5:

Prospering
Obedience Brings Blessings

- **Chapter 17** Choices & Consequences
- **Chapter 18** Choose Joy
- **Chapter 19** God's Grace
- **Chapter 20** Get In Where You Fit In

Chapter 17
Choices & Consequences

Do you remember the Deion Sanders and Jerry Jones commercial from way back in the day? It was advertising Pizza Hut's new meat lovers stuffed-crust pizza.[131] That pizza was fire, by the way! Deion's athletic career was at a high, when he was playing both baseball and football; while playing for the Dallas Cowboys, he played both offense and defense. Dion had just negotiated a new contract with the Cowboys that paid him an unreal amount of money for that time.

The commercial starts with Jerry Jones and Deion sitting in the stadium and Jerry asks him what he's going to play, football or baseball. Deion smiles and says, "Both, boss!" Then Jerry asks him if he's going to play offense or defense, and

---
131. "Both Boss" 1995 Pizza Hut Commercial. https://www.youtube.com/watch?v=MkhNZjTa6_M

again Deion replies–both! Then Jerry asks if Deion wants meat lovers or stuffed-crust pizza. Deion's reply lit up the Pizza Hut phone lines with thousands of people calling in to try this new pizza that Deion had just co-signed on. Then, they end the commercial with Jerry Jones asking what it's going to take to sign him: $15 or $20 million. To which Deion obviously replied–***both!*** That was a great commercial. It would be nice if all of the decisions we needed to make in life could be so easy.

Life is full of choices. Every single day we make big choices, little choices, choices about what to eat, what to wear, which way to turn, what time to leave work, who to be friends with, who to date, who to marry, whether to be grumpy or in a good mood, when to go to bed, and on and on and on. In fact, some sources suggest that the average person makes an eye-popping 35,000 choices per day.[132] As a part of being created in the image of God, we are given the precious gift of free will. This means we have the freedom to choose what we want to do.

However, a life lesson goes along with this wonderful gift of free will that God has blessed us with. I have endeavored to teach my kids and anyone else I have mentored throughout the years that life is all about choices and consequences. The simple fact in life is, if you make good choices, you will experience good consequences, but if you make bad choices, you will experience bad consequences. Choose wisely.

---

132. Eva M. Krockow, Ph.D, *Psychology Today*. "How Many Decisions Do We Make Each Day?," September 27, 2018. https://www.psychologytoday.com

PROSPERITY AFTER TURNING TO THE LORD

God used Moses to relay this message loud and clear to the nation of Israel. After God delivered the Israelites from bondage in Egypt, it wasn't long before they started to show their stubbornness and disobedience. Time and time again, God used Moses to let the people know they would be blessed if they obeyed the Lord's commands and cursed if they did not. He even outlined the many blessings they would receive: they would have many children, their crops would be plentiful, they would have much livestock, and the Lord would give them victory over any enemy that came against them. All they had to do was be obedient to Him and the Lord promised to bless everything they put their hands on.[133] Wow!

However, if they were not obedient, they shouldn't expect to prosper. In fact, God would curse them for being disobedient. He again lines out what the curses would be so they wouldn't be surprised. Women would have trouble having babies, their crops and livestock would be cursed, the Lord would cause confusion to come on them, their enemies would defeat them, and they would be plagued with diseases until they were destroyed.[134] No, thank you. Obedience seems like a better choice.

With the stakes being so high, you would think the people would get it and fall in line. You would only have to tell me once, right? Yeah, whatever. We can be just as stubborn and rebellious as the Israelites back then. We want to do the right thing, but doing the wrong thing seems so fun sometimes. We don't often think about the long-term consequences of

---
133. Deuteronomy 28:1–9, NIV.
134. Deuteronomy 28:15–25, NIV.

doing the wrong thing. Just like the Israelites we have our own struggle with sin. And this breaks God's heart.

WE ALL KNOW BETTER

We all know better, right? The Israelites heard the message loud and clear, proclaimed through Moses. God expected them to be obedient and in return, He would bless them. This is the same advice that King David passed along to Solomon. He wanted his son to be blessed by God and to rule over a prosperous kingdom. David knew this would require Solomon to be obedient to the Lord first. David knew that Solomon had witnessed how much his disobedience had cost him and he didn't want this for his son. No parent wants their kids to make the same mistakes they made. David made a lot of public errors along the way, but he learned from them. Now, he was passing his wisdom on to his son.

This wise advice still holds true for you and me today. I pray that all of my children watch me and think about how they can avoid some of the mistakes I have made in life. My wife and I do our best to engage our kids in many of our family discussions. We want them to see what we are doing and be able to ask questions so they can know the rationale behind the decisions we make. This isn't always convenient, and I'll admit, sometimes it can be downright annoying to have our kids all up in our business. Yet, this is the cost of instilling wisdom in them. Sure, it was easier when they were younger, because they would sit back and listen but not say anything.

When my youngest son Joshua was about five years old, my wife overheard him give "eavesdropping" advice to his four-year-old sister, Katie. These two have always been attached at the hip, although they try to pretend like they don't like each other. They are Irish twins, born about fifteen months apart. When the other three older boys were in school, Josh and Katie were still in the house with Ang; they loved to play together. By play, I mean they tried to control the movements, thoughts, and actions of each other. They are still this way, by the way. Anyway, one day Ang overheard Josh asking Katie, "Do you want to know my life's motto? Always be listening, but don't act like it." Too bad he doesn't still have that life's motto. Josh loves to add his two cents in every conversation he hears now.

THE OFFER OF LIFE OR DEATH

As a family, we have studied Deuteronomy 30, when Moses gave the offer of life and death to the Israelites. In this passage, God once again lays out the situation of choices and consequences. We could either choose life and prosperity, or death and destruction. Then He went on to convey that we make this choice by the way we choose to live. I highlight four points when I teach that passage:

> **1. We have a CALL to choose** *(Deuteronomy 30:11–14). God informed the Israelites that this wouldn't be a difficult choice for them, nor is it asking too much of them. He's not asking them to do something impossible, and He's not trying to make it confusing. He wants to make sure they are clear about what He is asking of them.*
> **2. We have a clear CHOICE to make** *(Deuteronomy 30:15). He presented His commands*

clearly and precisely so that the Israelites and all of His people would know and understand. He is also asking us if we want to have life and prosperity, or death and destruction.

3. We have CONSEQUENCES for the choice (Deuteronomy 30:15–18). *They could either be obedient to Him and have a full life with God's prosperity and blessing, or experience death and destruction as a result of disobedience.*

4. We have CONDITIONS for the correct choice (Deuteronomy 30:16). *We are given three conditions if we decide to choose life and prosperity. We are told we need to love God, walk in His ways, and keep His commands. Does that sound familiar? This is the same advice that David gives to His son when he is about to die,[135] and these are the main points of this book.*

God tells them what He wants them to choose. He tells them to choose life so that they and their children will be blessed (see Deuteronomy 30:19–20, NIV). I'm writing this book because I want to encourage you to choose life and prosperity, so you and your children will be blessed as well.

NEWTON'S LAW

I learned about Sir Isaac Newton's laws of motion in high school science class. Newton's Third Law of Science states that every action has an equal and opposite reaction.[136]

---

135. 1 Kings 2:1–3, NIV.
136. Editors of Britannica, "Newton's Laws of Motion," fact-checked March 23, 2023. https://www.britannica.com/science/Newtons-laws-of-motion.

When I was in college I studied philosophy and was again introduced to this theory as it relates to life and philosophy. For every cause, there is an effect, yada, yada, yada. I'm sure you remember.

The bottom line is: I believe this concept to be true. It's been tested and proven and rings the truest in practical life experience. Life is about the choices we make, both good and bad, and how these choices affect us, those around us, our friends, families and our kids for generations to come.

THE RICH KEEP GETTING RICHER

People who make good choices receive good consequences and good benefits. A lot of the choices you make today will affect your children's children. Look at the immigrants who came into Ellis Island. Because they made the choice and took the risk of getting on the boat to come to America, their families were changed for generations. Many immigrants went on to open businesses that their descendants still own and operate in New York, Pennsylvania, Chicago, and other locations.

Cornelius Vanderbilt, Joseph Kennedy, and Martin Luther King Jr., are examples of people who positively affected generations after them by the positive choices they made in life. There is a benefit to making wise decisions. Some people think about things and evaluate the risk and possible outcomes before they take action. We see many examples in finance, investing, handling credit, saving, and other areas.

You've heard the saying, "The rich just keep on getting richer." I believe this to be a true statement because the rich have learned to make wise choices from people around them who have learned to acquire wealth. As a result of making these wise choices, they do things that lead to more wealth. Often, the consequences of their good choices lead to them growing their fortune.

This also works in reverse. It sometimes seems like the poor just keep on getting poorer. This is often because the choices they make tend to focus on the pressing need in the moment. Many poor people haven't learned to look down the road and forecast what is coming that could affect them financially. So, they make their financial decisions based on their current situation. It's easy to do this, especially when your money is already tight, but it nevertheless leads to not-so-favorable consequences. As a teenager whose family was living one step out of the projects, my parents weren't knowledgeable enough to teach me how to make wise decisions concerning money. I made a few unwise financial choices early in life.

WHY, THANK YOU, MR. CHASE VISA!

In my junior year of high school, I applied for and received my first credit card. I had no idea what it really meant to have a credit card. Although I thought I was a fairly sharp person and did my best to be responsible, I had no idea about how important it was to maintain a good credit rating. No one talked to me about credit, spending, savings, or anything pertaining to making wise financial choices.

What enticed me to get this credit card was seeing that if I charged five hundred dollars' worth of stuff, it would only cost me eleven dollars per month. Eleven dollars didn't seem too overwhelming to me, especially since I was working part-time at McDonald's and making about seventy-five dollars a week. I knew I could handle that small payment, so I charged a pair of track shoes. They were bright yellow and blue Asics discus shoes that helped me glide across the discus ring a little smoother. At the time I was really into throwing the discus and was told that these shoes would help me throw it even farther. So, I charged them. *Side note:* they did help me win a lot of track meets and set a lot of records. I broke the school discus record that still stands today. Wassup, Macomb High School! When are you going to put a brotha in the Hall of Fame?

Anyway, charging those shoes was so easy that I decided to charge a Nike sweatshirt from Eastbay magazine. I had never owned a Nike sweatshirt before. Wow! A few CDs here, a gold necklace there, some gas for the good ole '72 pinto and the next thing you know, I owed Chase Visa five hundred dollars. In a few short weeks, I maxed out my credit card.

It wasn't a problem for a few months because I was making the minimum payment with ease. Even though I was consistently paying the minimum payment, I noticed the balance wasn't going down very much. The next thing I knew, football season rolled around and it was my senior year. I stopped working at McDonald's, so I had no income. I didn't have any savings. I had no money to pay the minimum payment. The late fees and finance charges really started to kick in.

I went to my mom for advice and she told me to send them what I could and write a letter of explanation. Let them know that I intended to pay but wasn't able to right now. Unfortunately, this didn't seem to stop Chase Visa from wanting their money.

Let me pause the story for a moment and offer a little side lesson that I have learned–we have to pay our bills! The consequence of choosing to not pay your bills is that the bill collectors will hound you until they get their cash. Trust me, I know! They don't care how young or old you may be, they don't care about your intentions or your situation, and they aren't interested in your letter telling them why you didn't pay. They just want their money and they will track you down and annoy you until they get it. Their motto is, "If you are old enough to charge, you are old enough to pay." That nugget of truth is free.

The same could be said for the payday loan shops today. I can't stress enough how much you should avoid these places. The interest rates are so high (over three hundred percent on average) that people cannot pay off their loans while covering normal living expenses. The typical borrower is compelled to take out one loan after another, incurring new fees each time out. This is the debt trap. Avoid these places all together.

So, Chase Visa kept calling and calling. This went on for a few months. They would call, and I would duck their calls. I kept sinking deeper into debt while trying to pay what I could. Finally, the summer after I graduated, I was able to settle accounts with them and pay what I owed in full. Fortunately, my credit didn't suffer too badly and I learned a valuable life lesson–I need to keep a steady job so that I can always make the minimum payment.

LESSON LEARNED–NOT

Fast forward a year later, I was in my sophomore year of college and I had a few more credit cards. Since I've always been a quick learner, I was holding true to my newfound life lesson of always making the minimum payment. At that time, in an effort to try and build a positive credit history, I had a few more credit cards with semi-manageable balances on each of them. I was proud that I had amicable business relationships with J.C. Penney's, Montgomery Ward's, Citibank Visa, and my old friend Chase Visa. Everything appeared to be going well and I was making the minimum payments each month. I was determined to be more disciplined and only charged the things I needed as a college student. Things like books, school supplies, and toiletries, and well . . . every now and then, while out on the town, I would charge an evening meal. Then once, I had to charge the new stereo equipment that I needed, a fly silk shirt, and that smooth leather coat. Just the basic *needs* of a college student.

Let me stop here and acknowledge what I'm sure you have already realized. I learned the wrong lesson about credit cards before. Let me get serious for a moment. Credit cards are serious business and need to be thought through before you get too comfortable using them. There's no such thing as free money and credit card companies are doing so well because many people have learned this the hard way. Most young people don't realize how high the interest really is and how quickly the late fees add up. I encourage you to think it through before you start frequently using your credit cards Adopt a plan for when and how you will use them. First of all, keep a steady job so you will be able to pay what you owe. Secondly, avoid using credit cards unless you absolutely have to. Then, do your best to pay them in full at the end of each month so you avoid the exorbitant fees.

I'm not suggesting that you should never use credit cards, because they are a good tool to help establish a good credit history when you learn to use them wisely. I know some people who use credits cards frequently each month to get the cash-back rewards or to collect frequent flier miles. They then pay off the cards at the end of each month to avoid finance charges. In these cases, the credit cards are being used to benefit the user and would be considered a wise choice. I highly recommend only using credit cards in case of an emergency, then pay the balance off as quickly as you can. A little common sense goes a long way.

Back to the story, where was I? Oh, yeah, my *needs*. With so many needs, I soon came to a point where I owed so much that I couldn't make the minimum payments and I began to default on my payments again. The reminder phone calls started coming in all over again. Soon they turned from reminder calls, to requests for payment calls, and then to "Why aren't you paying?" calls. This time I was getting this from four different companies waiting for what I owed them.

This was a very stressful time for me, having to deal with the pressures of school and with this financial situation. The sad part is that I had no one to blame but myself. My unwise choices put me into this predicament and now I was experiencing a negative consequence.

I was stressed, distracted, and embarrassed that the creditors were calling so much. They would call my dorm room in the morning, afternoon, and night asking for their money. They left messages with anyone who answered. "Have Alex call us about the money he owes." All of my friends knew that I was a poor, unwise failure who couldn't pay his bills.

The choices I made to indulge and buy things I wanted but could not afford led to consequences I didn't think of. I was being harassed by endless phone calls, socially embarrassed in front of my school mates, and my credit score was dropping every month. By the time I graduated from college my credit rating was in such bad shape that I couldn't buy a car or get an apartment. I often thought about how nice it would have been if I would have never opened that first credit card account. Life is much more simple when you learn to live within your means and only buy things you can afford. I wish I would have learned the real lesson about credit cards the first time.

SAVINGS AND USING CREDIT WISELY

Today, Ang and I have learned the value of saving. I teach my kids that savings gives you options. I would suggest living the type of life where you avoid buying all the shiny new stuff that all the commercials entice us to buy. And don't even try to keep up with the Jones. He's a doctor and makes ten times what you do! Live within your means and learn to be a disciplined saver.

However, in society today, I realize that at times we need credit. How many of us have $45,000 in cash to buy the car outright? Who among us can fork out the $250,000 upfront for that house we need to live in with our family? Not me. If this is you, I would like you to be my new friend.

The point is, avoiding credit isn't always the right choice. I believe using credit wisely is. Life is about making wise choices and receiving good consequences. Learn to do this by making choices, not avoiding them.

THINK LONG TERM

This is true in other areas of our life as well. The choices you make in the career you choose, or who your spouse will be, where you live, and the friends you choose will either lead to good consequences or bad ones. Learn to take time to evaluate things and think them through. Play out in your mind how the situation could possibly turn out. This is why I love the game of chess. It teaches players to think ahead and plan for the future. The best chess players are the ones who learn to think four, five, and six moves ahead. The exceptional players can think ahead and make their immediate choice of movement based on the consequences ten to twelve moves away. When you learn to think things through and evaluate all possible outcomes, you will learn to make better choices and your life will be better all around.

Be a mentally strong man who thinks about the consequences of all the choices he makes. Too many people want to be blessed and live a prosperous life, but they don't want to put in the work and live an obedient life. Nah, Bruh. Man UP and realize that obedience brings blessing.

Chapter 18
Choose Joy

In all things, choose joy.

On April 29, 2022, our lives changed forever. That was the night my 15-year-old son, Mason, was diagnosed with T-cell leukemia. He's still in the middle of fighting his cancer battle. I remember it like it was yesterday. Just before the day ended, we got a call from his school saying we should come pick him up. One of his teachers noticed he looked a little pale and was kind of short of breath. The previous weekend he had just finished dancing his heart out in a three-night production of "High School Musical." We were so proud that our little freshman boy actually got a speaking part. We picked him up from school and my wife indicated that she wanted to take him to urgent care. He'd been coughing for a couple of weeks, but we thought it was just allergies. We were way wrong.

As usual in the life of a big family, it was another busy night for us. My daughter Katie went to grandma's house, my son Joshua was in a school play at the junior school, and I had a men's conference to attend, so my wife took Mason to urgent care. After a brief exam, the doctor decided he didn't like Mason's cough and wanted to get a chest x-ray to rule out pneumonia. He said my wife should take him to Cox South, one of the big hospitals in our town. This was good with us because one of our best friends runs the urgent care there, although he wasn't there that night. Mason and Ang arrived at Cox South. They started running all kinds of tests, scans, and x-rays. That's when they found it. A mass the size of my fist was lodged in his chest.

I was called to the hospital while they were still running more tests. When I arrived the urgent care doctor greeted me by waving me back to his office while he was on the phone. He was frantically trying to make arrangements with another hospital in town for immediate treatment. While sliding the phone away from his ear to greet me, he started talking about Mason's white blood cell counts being elevated and they were going to get him to Mercy Hospital right away because Mercy is affiliated with St. Jude's Children Hospital…wah wah wah wah wah wah. That's all I heard after hearing St. Jude's. The doctor didn't know, but up to this point, I didn't have any details. I wasn't prepared to hear about white blood cell counts being elevated.

I stopped the doctor and said, "Wait! Hold up. Do you mean…" I paused because I couldn't bring myself to say the word. I remember him lowering the phone even more and looking at me with compassion in his eyes. He shook his head, but he didn't want to say the word either. I asked again, "So does that mean..." then the word came out " ... he has cancer?"

THE WAITING GAME

David was a teenager[137] when he was first anointed to be the next king of Israel, yet he didn't become king until he was thirty years old.[138] From the time he was anointed, David began preparing for the assignment. He became familiar with the palace when he spent time in King Saul's service playing the harp to soothe the king when he was tormented.[139] He found his courage on the battlefield when he bested the giant Goliath, winning a significant victory for the nation of Israel over the Philistines.[140] This was the beginning of many battles that David fought and won for his nation. He was proving himself to be a mighty warrior and the people sang songs about him, which made Saul very jealous.[141]

Saul plotted to kill David, sending him on the run to try to save his life. Some historians wrote that for nearly eight years David was on the run from Saul and escaped to Ziklag to avoid Saul's pursuit. That's a long time to be on the run fearing for your life. This must have been difficult for David to deal with. His emotions had to be up and down. Many of his feelings of despair are recorded in the Psalms. He believed he was hated without a cause, according to Psalm 69:4.

---

137. The fact that David was not yet serving in the army tells us he was definitely under 20 years old (see Numbers 1:3).
138. 2 Samuel 5:4, NIV.
139. 1 Samuel 16:14–20, NIV.
140. 1 Samuel 17, NIV.
141. 1 Samuel 18:6–9.

David knew what it felt like to have to wait for a promise to come to fruition. He waited some fifteen years to become king of Israel. I get frustrated when I have to wait a few months, weeks, or sometimes even hours. David could have taught graduate level classes on what it means to patiently wait on the Lord. Yet, wait he did. Through it all, he never wavered in his trust, obedience, and love for God. David taught us that waiting isn't doing nothing; David was busy while he was waiting.

GOD IS NEVER IN A HURRY

David learned that the Lord is not limited in time. He is sovereign, and a part of being sovereign is that He can do whatever He wants whenever He wants. He doesn't have to meet a deadline; His deadline is when He wants it to be. God doesn't have to meet a quota; He *is* the quota. His sense of time is nothing like our sense of time. The sooner we realize that, the sooner we will stop stressing over things that happen to us in our life. Peter tells us in 1 Peter 3:8 that a thousand years is like a day to Him. God isn't on our timetable, so we need to stop expecting Him to be. God's perfect plan is always on time and He promises that He will never leave us, nor forsake us.[142] He's going to take care of us, so we trust Him, and trust His timing.

Even though God had a reason for David's waiting doesn't mean that David understood or agreed with it. All throughout the Psalms, we see David crying out to God with this sort of question: "How long will this take, God?" We see this in passages like Psalm 13:1. I imagine at some point in your

---
142. Deuteronomy 31:8, NIV.

life you have asked God this exact question. But be assured, there is a reason God has you in the "waiting room." For David, God wanted to see how he responded to trouble, if He could trust David, how David led men in battles, and probably many other things. It is the same with us. God must see how we handle and respond to situations before He gives us the "seat" that we desire to be in.[143] Once you have decided to believe this, spend your time trying to wait on God with the right attitude.

Just as God tested David's faith while he waited to become king, God will test our faith as well. David endured a lot of trials, pain, and suffering during his lifetime. Through it all he proclaimed, "The Lord is my strength and shield. I trust him with all my heart. He helps me, and my heart is filled with joy. I burst out in songs of thanksgiving (Psalm 28:7, NLT). This was His message for Solomon and for us.

EASIER SAID THAN DONE

We have to choose to be people full of joy. The Bible says in 1 Thessalonians 5:16: "be joyful always." God intends for us to be joyful all throughout this life. God knows that we will experience tough times in our lives. He knows that sometimes things just won't go our way and He realizes that we won't always feel good. Yet, He still gives us the instruction to always be joyful. This could cause many of us to think this was an unrealistic expectation considering all the junk we have to deal with in life.

---

143. Ben Hjalmer, "Wait For It," Woodfields Baptist Church Blog, January 15, 2018. https://woodfieldsbaptist.org/2018/01/wait-for-it/

Surely God knows how hard it is for us men to balance all the demands for our time and energy. Surely He knows how expensive it is to pay for our house, car, insurance, groceries, the kids sports, clothes, braces, and all the other things competing for our money. Doesn't he realize the stress we are under sometimes? Surely He notices all the people coming at us trying to bring drama and strife into our lives–boss, coworkers, neighbors, family members. A brotha's not trying to be all smiles all the time.

Moreover, being the sovereign God that I know Him to be, surely He foreknew all the pain that would flood my heart, mind, and soul when I received that gut punch on April 29th. His Word says that He knows everything.[144] So, He knew we would experience setbacks from time to time and even suffer loss during our lifetime. We don't have to tell God that sometimes being a man is pretty darn difficult. He, of all people, knew we would face trials and heartaches of many kinds. Therefore, how does He expect us to always be joyful?

GRUMPY NO MORE

Have you ever met a Christian who was just grumpy all the time? They were mean and negative, and usually looked for and expected the worst in every situation. These people think they are just being realistic about things and don't even realize their negative attitude. They don't understand the lack of joy in their life. No one around them would mistake them for being happy although they may think they are. Their actions speak louder than their words. It's easy to see they are living without joy in their life. They love God and they are still a

---
144. Psalm 139:1-24, NIV; 1 John 3:20, NIV.

Christian, but they are not obeying what the Word tells them concerning joy.

Angie's grandmother struggled with maintaining her joy. It was hard for her to focus on the positive things in life and she was given to being depressed. She was a wonderful Christian woman, who was very loving and would do anything for her church family. She was faithful to the Lord and to the church, yet she struggled with being joyful. For as long as I knew her, this was the case. I would often tease her and joke with her to try to get her to smile and laugh. Sometimes it would work but most of the time she would scold me and say, "Alex, I'm going to tell your mother on you." I enjoyed trying to bring a smile to her face.

I couldn't understand why she wasn't happy more often. I mean, she had a lot of good things happening in her life: she had a family who loved her and cared for her. Her church family was very supportive of her and accommodating to her needs. People from our church would pick her up each week and bring her to service anytime she wanted. Oftentimes, our youth pastor and other people from the church would get her dinner and deliver it to her, sometimes staying for hours just to visit with her. From the outside, it appeared she had every reason in the world to be joyful.

I can remember one year, shortly after Angie and I were married, Dora came to visit with us and stayed for a week. This was a big deal as she was getting older and Angie realized this might be the last time her grandmother would be able to stay with us. During that visit, I had the opportunity to talk with her several times about all kinds of stuff. I asked her why she wasn't more joyful. She explained to me that she felt lonely and helpless. She didn't like living in her apartment by herself and, although Angie's mom and sister visited her nearly every day, she longed for more time with them.

We talked about the situation she was in. I pointed out that although she wasn't wealthy, all her needs were being met. I pointed out that, although she was advancing in age and wasn't as mobile as she used to be, she could still get around on her own. She still had good use of her mind and was good at doing puzzles to stimulate her brain. She had some sort of social contact with numerous people every day–people from the church, from her family, and other friends. She couldn't deny that people were always visiting her.

Dora was listening to me closely, I could tell. I played a song for her by contemporary Christian singer Larnelle Harris and as she listened to the words, I could see the tears forming in her eyes. The song is called "I Choose Joy" and the lyrics are powerful:

I choose joy
I'll never let the problems keep me down
Cause the Lord is working all things out
For my good
I choose joy

To tell the truth, this world is full of trouble
And if we live long enough it's sure to come our way
We've a choice to walk in fear and trembling
Or claim the victory that's already ours this very day.

Choose Joy

I choose joy
I'll never let the problems keep me down
Cause I know the Lord will work things out
For my good
I choose joy

So when I wake and stumble to the mirror
And what I see makes me wish
That I could stay in bed
There's a power deep within my being
And it commands my soul to start
Praising the Lord with every breath

So when I find myself under a load
Of circumstances and care
God wants to know
What I'm doing under there

I choose joy, I choose joy
I'll never let the problems keep me down
'Cause I know the Lord will work things out
For my good, I choose joy . . . [145]

This was one of the most special moments I had with Dora. As she cried, she began to realize that for years she had not been choosing joy. Instead, she chose to let her feelings and emotions dictate her actions. We talked about how the Bible tells us to think about things that are good, right, noble, and praiseworthy. I challenged her to focus her thoughts on all

---
145. Larnelle Harris, "I Choose Joy," Track 1 on *I Choose Joy* album. Benson, 1992, CD.

the good things in her life and on the many blessings God had given her. When we do this, it's easy for us to choose joy!

WHEN I THINK ABOUT THE LORD

I want to challenge you to right now stop and think about all the things that God has done for you. Maybe you just make a mental list or maybe you want to write some of your blessings down in your journal. Seriously, put this book down and just spend a few moments reflecting on all the good things in your life.

Whenever I take the time to do this, the old, simple song "When I Think about the Lord," comes to mind. If you are like me, once a song pops in my head, it will remain on my mind until I sing it completely through, bridge and all. I'm serious. I won't be able to clearly hold another thought until I get the song out. So, let's take another break and let it out:

> When I think about the Lord,
> How He saved me, how He raised me,
> How He healed me to the uttermost,
> How He filled me with the Holy Ghost.
>
> When I think about the Lord,
> How He picked me up and turned me around
> How He placed my feet on solid ground.
> It makes me want to shout,
>
> Hallelujah, thank You Jesus, Lord you're worthy

Choose Joy

Of all of the glory, of all the honor, and all of the praise. [146]

Choosing joy is a conscious decision that flows out of what you choose to think about and focus on. A part of obeying the Lord and becoming the man that He wants us to be is to consistently choose joy. No matter what happens to you in life, no matter what you are going through, no matter how you feel, and no matter how tough life is right now–decide to be a joyful person.

When you think about all the good things the Lord has done for you and about all He has given you–life, family, friends, clothes, food, breath, and more–it should make you realize how good you have it right now. Especially since we live in America. We are so blessed to live in this great country. We should definitely thank the Lord for all that we have. I've had the privilege to travel to over a dozen different countries, and every time I couldn't wait to return back to the U.S.A. People are lining up to try to come to our great country, and in spite of the few flaws we may have, I wouldn't trade living in this great country for any other one.

Nevertheless, when we think about all the blessings we have in life it should make us want to give thanks. Consider being joyful in the midst of all your many blessings. Gratitude flows from a joyful heart.

I'm reminded of the question I saw posted on Facebook a while back: "What if the only things you carried into tomorrow were the things that you thanked God for today?" Friends, what would you carry into tomorrow? Does your lack of joy

---

146. Christ For The Nations Music, James Huey."When I Think About the Lord," ©1998 CFN Music.

stop you from seeing all the good things you have in your life? Does a lack of joy rob you from counting your blessings?

If for no other reason, choose to be joyful because the Lord is good to you. He is compassionate and gracious and longs to give you good gifts. He is near to all who call on Him so you are never alone. He's a friend to all who are lonely. He'll stick closer than a brother. He's always there in your time of need, and He'll never leave you nor forsake you. He has the power of life and death in His hand, and yet, He knows everything you are thinking and all that you are going through. He's the Alpha and Omega, the creator of the universe, and He cares enough to provide you with every one of your needs. All that God asks in return is that you have a joyful heart.

WHAT YOU LEARN WHILE WAITING

I began this chapter talking about my son's cancer battle. As I'm writing this he is not out of the woods. Far from it. It's been just over a year since his diagnosis and, praise the Lord, he has been declared cancer free. Although the cancer is in remission, we are in the middle of a two-year treatment protocol that requires him to have weekly chemotherapy infusions. The survival rate for this form of T-cell leukemia is ninety-six percent when Mason goes through the entire treatment. I've said that statement many times, yet it still is sobering to have to think about a survival rate for my teenager. Teenage boys shouldn't have to think about their mortality at this stage in life–they should still believe they are invincible. But that's not the case for Mason. He's well aware of what's at stake.

He's also no stranger to the constant pain and suffering that cancer brings. He endures the physical pain of being poked and prodded every time he goes to the hospital, which is usually a couple times each week. He has to deal with the nausea and vomiting, pain in his joints, constant fatigue, and the noticeable changes to his body and hair. Then he endures the mental and emotional pain and suffering of being away from his friends and having to miss school. Since he's neutropenic most of the time, this means he's highly susceptible to picking up other people's germs, so we have to keep him isolated. So basically, he has to be away from his friends, schoolmates, and activities for two to three years. What would that do to your spirit? It's kicking his butt.

At times like this, we have to be ready to stand on what we believe. From the very beginning, I never once tried to make this battle seem like something that it wasn't. We acknowledge all the time that ***cancer sucks!*** Because it does. Yet, we talk with Mason about seeking the Lord to see what He wants Mason to get from this whole experience.

From the very beginning, Mason said God told him that He was going to use this experience for two purposes: 1) to teach Mason patience, and 2) to draw him closer to God. It absolutely stinks to see your son suffering through this long, painful cancer journey, but to know that God is speaking to my son brings joy to my heart. That's all that a dad can ask for. Our family knows that God is working things out for Mason's good, and we trust Him.

Suffering stinks. There's nothing else to be said about it. However, even in the midst of your suffering, God will give you the grace and the strength to Man UP and still be able to choose joy. This is a little more easy to accept when we consider there is a purpose for suffering. Before I go into that,

I want to be clear. I do not believe God causes us to suffer. He only has good things in mind for us. Suffering is not a sign that we've been forsaken; rather, it's a sign that we live in a world that doesn't function the way God intended and is in need of a Savior.[147]

PURPOSE FOR SUFFERING

A friend gave us a book that has been a big help for me in the midst of Mason's cancer journey. The book is called *Suffering* by author and pastor, Paul David Tripp. He acknowledged that God doesn't always answer our specific why questions, but it does reveal why God allows hardships in the lives of His children. He offers four purposes for our suffering that I will summarize:

> *1.* **We suffer because we live in a fallen world** *(2 Corinthians 4:7–10). Tripp says that suffering is the normal experience of every person living between the fall of Adam and Eve and the future second coming of Christ. God created us cracked and fragile because He wants to accomplish something good through our fragility.*
> *2.* **We suffer because God uses it to produce good in us** *(James 1:2–4). Suffering in the hands of God is a powerful tool of personal growth and transformation. It exposes some of the bad things inside of us. In our pain, we're mean, grouchy, impatient, demanding, irritable, and angry. God knows we*

---

147. Paul David Tripp, *Suffering: Gospel Hope When Life Doesn't Make Sense.* (Wheaton, IL: Crossway, 2018).

need eternal changes and He often uses hard tools to produce sturdy hearts.

3. **Suffering prepares us for how God will use us** *(2 Corinthians 1:3–9). God uses our suffering to help make us aware of, willing and ready to comfort others. I saw this first hand when my dad died. Before I experienced it myself, I was empathetic to what others felt who lost a parent. After my own dad died, I understood. I became more aware of other people's pain and suffering in their time of loss.*

4. **Suffering teaches us that this world is not our final home** *(2 Corinthians 4:16–5:5). Heaven is. God uses suffering to release us from the hope that this present world will ever be the paradise that our hearts long for. We must not get too comfortable here.*

FROM THE FIELDS TO THE PALACE

Suffering helped David grow from being the lowly shepherd boy and transformed him into the mighty warrior king of Israel. David learned, grew, and developed while he was on the run suffering. He became a wise and patient political leader who knew how to unite a kingdom. He became a strong man of God who trusted the Lord and was committed to obeying His commands.

David became a well-rounded man, who grew his giftings in music and writing. David paid his dues by tending the flock, one of the lowliest jobs in all Israel. He was willing to risk his life for his family, for his nation, and for a cause bigger than himself. Along the way, he learned to obey God's commands, testifying to the truth that obedience brings blessing. Although it's never the chosen path, suffering produced great results in David's life. He wrote in Psalms 46:1–2, "God is our refuge and strength, an ever-present help in trouble. Therefore we will not fear."

Can you imagine being able to go anywhere and do anything without fearing? As a man, that should put a smile on your face and cause you to choose joy. This is a part of the Man UP journey. I never said it would all be easy, but it is worth it.

Chapter 19
God's Grace

The grace of God is amazing. We don't deserve it, we can't understand it, yet God gives it to us as one of His greatest gifts. Most people are unaware of the different kinds of grace mentioned in the Bible. John Wesley taught on the three aspects of grace: *prevenient grace*, which is God's active presence in people's lives before they even sense the divine at work in their lives; *justifying grace*, through which all sins are forgiven by God; and *sanctifying grace*, which allows people to grow in their ability to live like Jesus.[148]

God offers us different kinds of grace to help us, no matter what situation we are in. When we have loved ones who don't know the Lord, we are praying prayers of what Wesley calls prevenient grace. We want God to reveal himself to them

---

148. Kenneth L. Carder, "A Wesleyan understanding of grace." https://www.resource-umc.org/en/content/a-wesleyan-understanding-of-grace

and turn their hearts towards Him. Then, we sing about His "amazing grace," which Wesley calls justifying grace, that offers us forgiveness of our sins. That's the grace that saved a wretch like me. Even though we don't deserve His grace, He offers it freely. And it's for our benefit, not His. We all deserve to be punished for our sins, yet He offers us forgiveness. Finally, the grace we are mainly talking about in this book is what Wesley would call God's sanctifying grace. That's the grace that gives us the power and ability to Man UP and live obedient lives that honor God.

Paul talked about this kind of grace when he wrote about the thorn in his flesh that he asked God to get rid of. God responded by telling Paul that His grace was sufficient for him and that His power is made perfect in weakness (1 Corinthians 12:8–9, NIV). I'm thankful that God offers us the kind of grace that enables us to live the life He has called us to live. We would never be able to measure up in our own strength. However, because God gives us His grace, we have the opportunity to prosper in this life and for all of eternity.

GOD'S AMAZING GRACE

For the majority of this chapter, I want to focus on God's justifying grace. I dare say all of us know people who are lost and need Jesus in their life. Prevenient grace prepares us for justifying grace. "Justification," said Wesley, "is another word for pardon. It is the forgiveness of all our sins, and . . . our acceptance with God."[149]

---

149. John Wesley, "The Scripture Way of Salvation" (Sermon, Aldersgate Street on May 24, 1738).

I've been in ministry for a number of years and have had the honor of leading many people to Jesus. It's always amazing to see the miracle of salvation, and it's such a blessing when you get to play a part in the process. Although I've witnessed it thousands of times, it never grows old. I can recall many special occasions of seeing people come to know the Lord.

I've witnessed altars full of over five hundred students giving their hearts to the Lord at a back-to-school rally in Florida. I've seen hundreds of people raise their hand for salvation during an open-air crusade in Venezuela. I've seen a room full of grown men crying ugly tears as they gave their heart to the Lord in a service I preached in a jail. I've also had the privilege of leading people to the Lord in my home, then baptizing them in the pool in the backyard. Each of them has a story of how God's grace met them where they were and captured their heart. It's so cool every single time.

I love seeing God's justifying grace at work. Perhaps the most memorable story that I witnessed firsthand was during the passing of my grandmother–Catherine Hall. Everyone who loved her called her "Cat." The story of how my grandmother accepted the Lord on her deathbed is the epitome of amazing grace.

THE STORY OF CAT

I was pretty much raised by my grandmother from the time I was born until I was about six years old. My mother was sixteen years old and unmarried when she got pregnant with me. Needless to say, because my mother was so young when she had me, my grandmother played a big part in raising me. Truth be told, I thought she was my mom for the first few years of my life. We lived in a small, two-bedroom house on 15th Street in Fort Pierce, Florida. My aunt Kaye and her four children also lived with us. And, sometimes, my uncle Joey would stay there and crash on the couch. Years later I was able to visit and walk through and I couldn't help but wonder how we all fit in that little two-bedroom house. But we made it work.

My aunt Kaye and her four kids (Trina, Dawn, Kim and Cedrick) all slept in one bedroom; Cat, my mom, and I were all in the other bedroom. Sometimes when my mom wasn't around, I remember my oldest cousin, Trina, sleeping in the other bed in the room with Cat and me. I'm not certain of how the sleeping arrangements were figured out back then. I do know that for the first few years of my life I shared a small twin-sized bed with my Grandmother Cat. We would both sleep on our sides, spooning. I would throw my leg across her back and rest comfortably as she laid as still as a mouse, sacrificing her own comfort for mine.

I was so spoiled too. Oftentimes, Cat would get up in the middle of the night to my cry asking for a glass of milk with a little sugar in it. It was like she was at my beck and call. Just before bed, she and I would walk across the street to Mrs. Versie's house, so I could buy a couple of vanilla sandwich cookies. Mrs. Versie sold those cookies two for a dime or five for twenty-five cents. Any time I would ask, Cat would provide the money and the safe passage for me to walk across 15th Street and get my normal snack. She was kind and generous and absolutely unaware of the consequences to my health later on in life. But that's beside the point.

Many afternoons, Cat would accompany me to the mango tree in our back yard to help me pick the mangoes that were too high for me to reach. We took trips around town every Thursday–*payday*. We would pick up her check from the laundry factory she worked, then stop at the neighborhood gas station to fill up the car. Every time, without fail, and usually without me having to ask, Cat would get me a honey bun. The kind with the white icing on top–those were and still are my favorite. Again, can you see why I was an offensive lineman? We would then go to McDonald's for dinner, or sometimes Cat would get Long John Silver's instead. Since I didn't like seafood, she would always make sure I got my cheeseburger Happy Meal without onions.

Cat would take me fishing in the canal behind the school, Francis K. Sweet, right next to our house. She would fish with a bamboo pole and could always catch a bunch of fish. Cat would cook Vienna sausages, rice, and creamed corn, and made the meanest pork chops ever. She was there for birthdays, Christmases, and every other day for the first five years of my life. She never let anyone lay a hand on me, even when I was bad and probably needed to be disciplined. My cousins often resented me because I was the youngest and treated like the baby of the house. I had the eye of my grandmother and they all knew I was her favorite. She was a wonderful grandmother.

EVERYTHING EXCEPT CHURCH

I did most things with Cat, except I never remember her taking us to church. My church years didn't start until after we moved to Illinois, halfway across the country from Cat.

Looking back, I realize that Cat didn't live a Christian life. My family used to say she loved three things; her Budweiser beer, her Salem regular cigarettes (Not the long cigarettes either. You didn't want to be caught bringing her the long ones), and her male grandchildren. In retrospect, I can see she lived a hard life, but I didn't know it at the time.

As I mentioned before, my aunt Kaye and my four cousins lived in the house with us so they were around for most of my childhood memories. Until I moved away from Florida for good when I was about seven years old, my Aunt Kaye was very instrumental in helping raise me. It was as though Cat was my mom but my Aunt Kaye was there raising her four kids. I really didn't know anything else.

I FOUND GOD IN ILLINOIS

I can still remember the big move to Illinois. My mom met a guy and moved us away from beautiful sunny Florida to live with this guy I had never met in freezing cold Illinois. He didn't even have his own place. We moved into his mother's house with him and his four other brothers and sisters. It was once again crowded in this new place and it was hard being so far away from Cat. Even then, because of how far we were apart, I knew my relationship with Cat would never be the same.

While in Illinois, my mom was creating a new life for us and eventually Christ would be the center of that new life. Every Sunday my mom would make me walk out of the projects and down the block to Mount Calvary Church of God in Christ. Even though she wasn't going, she made sure I was there every Sunday morning. Then and there, I started to learn about Jesus Christ for the first time.

Every Sunday morning, the youth Sunday school teacher, Mother Coleman, would greet me at the door and give me a great big ole hug and say, "Baby, Mother Coleman loves you and God loves you and He has a plan for your life." Then she would give me a piece of candy for remembering the memory verse. Week after week, every time I walked through the door, she was there to greet me. And every week, she would tell me she loved me and God loved me, and that He had a plan for my life. Somewhere along the line, I started to believe her. Mother Coleman introduced me to Jesus and I gave my heart to Him. Things would never be the same. Even at a young age, I realized that God's grace is *awesome*; it was enough to save my soul.

The people in the church taught me to pray for my mom's salvation. Pastor and Ms. Starling, Mother Clark, and Mother Coleman would join me in praying for my whole family to get saved. I was no more than eight or nine years old when I would stand in front of the whole congregation and testify about the things God had done for me. I had all the saints believing with me that Barbara Huston and my grandmother Cat would soon come to know the Lord. It wasn't long until my mom came to a revival service and gave her heart to the Lord. She has never looked back and is now one of the most godly women I know. She's the prayer support for our family and our ministry.

The next on my salvation hit list was my grandmother Cat. For years, I prayed for her without ceasing. I knew she would come to know the Lord but I didn't know when and where. As the years passed I graduated from junior high, started my football career, graduated from high school and college, and even got married, but Cat still hadn't surrendered her heart to the Lord. In fact, it appeared that she was falling further into her sinful lifestyle. We talked frequently about a lot of different things, but we never fully spoke about the Lord. She never, never wanted to go there.

I had a few opportunities to talk with her about my relationship with Christ and what He meant to me. She knew I was a Christian and she knew how much I wanted her to give her heart to the Lord, but she never really wanted to talk about it. She did her best to avoid having this conversation and when I would bring it up, she would smile and ignore what I would say about the Lord.

Cat kept growing older but never grew closer to the Lord. Her body was starting to break down and she developed heart problems. She suffered a stroke and a mild heart attack, but through it all, never surrendered her heart to the Lord. By the time she was in her mid-sixties, her body was really beat up and ready to quit on her because of smoking and drinking all her life. She could have died at any time and would have deserved the punishment that her lifestyle would have brought her–a life eternally separated from God in hell. *But,* God's grace is awesome.

MERCY SAID NO

In August 1999, my family found out that Cat had cancer throughout her body, with big tumors in her lungs and on her liver. It didn't look good at all. She knew she was sick, but she didn't want to know the extent of her sickness and didn't want to talk about it. The doctors told our family she only had months to live and there was nothing they could do. The cancer was too widely spread and her body couldn't take any form of treatment because it was in such bad shape.

Most of our family wanted to keep this news from her and just make her comfortable in her last few months on earth. Some of our family, the born-again believers who had been praying for her for years, realized the urgency of the situation. Cat needed to know she didn't have much more time to be reconciled with the Lord. We wanted her to know she was dying so she would at least get her soul right with God before she met Him face to face. All the opinions didn't really matter, because Cat knew what was going on; she just didn't want to talk about it.

I lived in Springfield, Missouri, at the time and made plans to visit Cat for what I knew could very well be the last time I would see her alive. The most economical flight I could find was out of Kansas City, Missouri, which is about a three-hour drive from Springfield. I would be doing a lot of driving so I needed music for this trip. I pulled out a CD I had bought six months earlier, but I had never listened to it. I don't know why I bought it and let it sit for so long, but that's when I discovered the song, "Mercy Said No" by Greg Long for the very first time. It was like God specifically orchestrated me discovering that song on that CD for this specific time.

As I drove to the airport in Kansas City, I listened to that song over and over on repeat. The lyrics spoke directly to my heart and made me do the ugly cry; I listened some more.

"Mercy said no,

I'm not gonna let you go.
I'm not gonna' let you slip away,
you don't have to be afraid.

Mercy said no,
  sin will never take control.
Life and death stood face to face,
  darkness tried to steal my heart away, but Mercy said no."[150]

God was letting me know, before I even got to Florida, that He was in control and that my years of praying would be answered. I knew Cat would be saved and I would see her again some day after both of our lives here on earth were over.

I had planned to be in Florida for a week and spent most of my time with Cat in her room. I wasn't prepared to see her in such bad shape. The hard life that she had lived had finally caught up with her. Cancer had spread throughout her body and she was in a lot of pain. She would go in and out of consciousness most of the time and was barely coherent. She couldn't really eat and she was restricted to her bed. She was just waiting to die. Sometimes I would hear her scream out, "Oh Jesus, please help me," and then she would grimace and try to endure the pain. She wasn't ready to let go of life because she knew she wasn't ready to meet her Maker.

For hours I would sit beside her bed and listen to gospel music with her and try to talk to her about the Lord. Many times, I asked her directly if she wanted to accept Jesus Christ

---

150. "Mercy Said No" lyrics © Capitol CMG Publishing, Universal Music Publishing Group, Warner Chappell Music, Inc.

as her personal Lord and Savior, but she would just get tears in her eyes and say no. She didn't think she was worthy. She thought she was too big a sinner and had done too many bad things during her lifetime. She didn't think God wanted her.

After spending a week with her, praying for her, talking with her, and singing songs with her, the time came for me to leave. I didn't really have peace about the situation. I was disappointed that things hadn't turned out the way I expected them to–the way that I prayed for them to. I just knew and believed with all my heart that she would get right with the Lord that week. I envisioned being there as she said the sinner's prayer and leaving her for the last time knowing for sure I would see her again in heaven one day. But, it never happened.

The next few weeks, while back home in Springfield, I kept in constant contact with my family in Florida. I had frequent conversations with my Aunt Kaye about what was happening. She would tell me about how Cat would wake up in the middle of the night screaming, "I'm not ready to go." Near the end, Cat had dreams that demons were coming to get her in the night. The Bible says that the devil comes only to steal, kill, and destroy,[151] and was battling to have her soul. I prayed even harder!

A couple weeks after my visit, my mom took a trip to Florida and spent time with Cat just before she passed. While my mom was there, the pastor of one of my cousin's would visit the house every night and have a time of prayer and worship with Cat. Through these times, and only a week before she passed, God's grace and mercy penetrated Cat's heart and

---
151. John 10:10.

she gave her heart to the Lord. I'm so thankful that only one week before she died, she finally yielded to Him.

She lived a hard life–she drank, cussed, and smoked. Sin was deeply rooted inside of her heart and she had strong feelings of guilt and unworthiness that she could not release on her own. The Lord was the only one who could help her and save her soul. I've often wondered why He did though. She didn't acknowledge Him her whole life. Some could question why God chooses to offer His grace and mercy to people who reject Him their whole lives. The only reason I can think of is because His grace is awesome!

GOD'S GRACE IS AWESOME

He extended grace to my beloved grandmother, Cat, only days before she departed this earth. She was a lifetime sinner who finally offered her heart to the Lord in the final days of her life–the 11th hour. It's because of this awesome grace that He extends the offer of forgiveness of our sins to all of us. If you think about it, none of us really deserve His grace. We've already mentioned how the Bible says in Romans 3:23: "For all have sinned and fallen short of the glory of God." This means we all have missed the mark that He set for us and as a result, we deserved to be punished. The punishment He set aside for sinners is an eternity apart from Him, being tormented in hell. Words can't describe that pain.

But God doesn't want this for you or anyone. The Bible also says that *it's His will that none should perish*.[152] He doesn't want anyone to spend eternity suffering apart from Him.

---

152. 2 Peter 3:9, NIV.

Isaiah 30:18, NIV, tells us that God "longs to be gracious to you" and He rises to show you compassion.

God's grace is awesome and He longs to extend it to you. Don't wait to accept His offer of grace! Don't take the chance and wait until the 11th hour like Cat did. Although it worked out for her, don't assume you can put off accepting His offer of grace with the same result. If God is speaking to your heart right now, I want to encourage you to Man UP and respond to His voice. Accept His grace today and realize how awesome He truly is. There is no better way to make sure you prosper now and for all of eternity.

Chapter 20
Get In Where You Fit In

I've been a Christian pretty much all of my life. Jesus touched my heart at a great school and I gave my life to Him. I've never looked back. I have very few moments in my life in which I have blatantly disobeyed what I know is His will for my life. Don't get me wrong, while I was in high school I had my knucklehead moments where I gave into my own youthful desires of sin and stepped outside of His plan for my life. But I never walked away from Him. I'm thankful that I had a family and church community who were quick to call me out on my sin and call me back to repentance. I definitely don't think I'm better than anyone else, but I really do try to obey the Lord's commands in the Bible so I can walk in His blessings.

My wife and I have prayed that each of our kids never walk a day outside of God's plan for their life. We have made it a priority to intentionally teach them what God's Word says and we make it a family expectation for all the Bryants to obey God's Word. We stand on the promises of God when He tells us to train up children in the way they should go; when they are old they will not depart from His ways.[153] We have worked hard to create a family culture that puts God at the center of everything we do, and just as iron sharpens iron we make sure to sharpen each other.

That's the story of my family. I don't say any of that to brag, because it's only by the grace of God that we are able to walk our faith journey this way. What about you? How is your faith journey? How are you leading your family?

When we started this journey together I mentioned that my original intent for writing this book was to instruct my kids. This is for them and for their children. I pray that it is a blessing to you and your family as well. The Lord has blessed me in so many ways and He has enriched my life. Now, I believe He has called me to be a blessing to you by sharing the wisdom in this book. The reality is that God blesses in different capacities, sometimes based on merit–and sometimes not. It all really reminds us that He is a God who has a big plan that we don't always understand, but we always know to be good, pleasing, and perfect, even if we don't seem to get an equal size of the pie.

Truth be told, none of us deserve any of God's blessings at all–and yet so readily He gave us all life, provision, and even His own Son Jesus Christ. Because He is a good God,

---

153. Proverbs 22:6.

He continues to pour out His goodness on us even when we don't always obey. Sure, others might receive more blessings, while some others receive less. But that's not the point. The point is that we were all once empty-handed, but we've now all received more than what we really deserve. If that's not grace, then I don't know what is.

WHO AM I, O LORD?

At the end of his life, King David may have had the same thoughts. However, he learned something that he wanted to pass along to his son, Solomon. I have attempted to pass that along to you. The formula for prospering is to be strong and act like a man, be observant and learn the Lord's commands, be faithful and walk in obedience, and endure by continuing to obey His commands–then you will prosper.

David had committed gross sin with Bathsheba, Uriah's wife. After he lusted for her, he committed adultery with her. To cover up the sin, he had Uriah killed and took Bathsheba to be a highly favored wife among his many others.

For about a year or more, David was able to hide that which was done in secret. Apparently, he thought he had gotten away with it. No one dared to question the king. Life went on as usual and all seemed to be well. That is until the prophet came and confronted David with his sin.

Maybe you can identify with David. I mean, you haven't taken a brotha's wife and committed a government conspiracy to have him killed, but you aren't living the way you know you should. The cool thing is that if you have missed the mark in the past, God won't hold that against you, if you ask Him for forgiveness. No matter what's going on in your life right now you can still start prospering. No matter if you have turned your back on the Lord, or if you have never before asked Him to be the Lord of your life, you can still get in on this great deal. Salvation is available to you right now. Get in where you fit in.

All you have to do is humble yourself, ask Him for forgiveness, and give Him your heart. Once you get that straight, start reading the Bible and doing what it says. He has so many instructions that He offers to teach you how to live like the godly man that He wants you to be.

Learn from David; he knew what it was like to fail. He failed in his marriage, with his kids, and in his community. We can see so many holes in his leadership on every level. Yet he never stayed there. Those things were not his legacy. After he dropped the ball, he went on to be known as a man after God's own heart. David's life proves that failure is not final. Sure he made a lot of mistakes along the way, but he learned from them and then passed his words of wisdom along to his son.

That same wisdom is good enough for all of us today. It's not what you did before you failed that determines if you are going to live a prosperous life. It's what you do after you fail. I hope that you've gathered this. When you fail, and believe me you will, humble yourself, quickly repent, and get back to being obedient to the Lord's commands.

God forgave David for everything he had done and then started to bless him immensely. God loves you just as much as He loved David. The same grace and goodness that He had for David, He extends to you today. David wrote about God's goodness when he said, "Who am I, O Sovereign LORD, and what is my family, that you have brought me this far?"[154] When you Man UP, you will feel the same way.

NO SHORTCUTS

But you have to be willing to put in the work. Blessings follow obedience. That's the way it works. You have to put in the work before you expect to prosper. Too many men want to skip to the end to receive the blessings without putting in the work of being obedient. They want God to be faithful to them without being faithful to Him. That's like expecting to have rock hard abs without ever going to the gym. Or, like having a strong marriage without investing in your relationship. Like wanting to be financially secure without being wise with your money. I guess it happens sometimes for some people. I guess some people are born with naturally good genes, some relationships don't have conflict, and some people win the lottery–but that's not the norm. That's not the case for you, my guy! You have to expect to put in the work.

To grow, you must have room to grow. In order to have time to learn what God commands of you, you may have to cut something else out of your schedule, or maybe just take a break from it for a while. Craig Groeschel, in his book *Lead Like It Matters*, says that sometimes you need to cut back in order to move forward.[155] Ask yourself what you are doing that doesn't directly contribute to helping you put yourself in a position to know God's Word more? The answer to that question needs to be eliminated. This may mean that you will have to say no to some things. Warren Buffet said, "The

---
154. 2 Samuel 7:18, NLT.
155. Craig Groeschel, *Lead Like It Matters: 7 Leadership Principles for a Church that Lasts* (Grand Rapids, MI: Zondervan, 2022).

difference between successful people and really successful people is that really successful people say no to almost everything."[156]

IT'S NOT ONLY ABOUT YOU

We must remember, our obedience, our growth, and our prosperity is not only about us. God wants to use you to impact other people. As men, we have responsibilities to our family, our job, our churches, and our community. There is a lot riding on you becoming the godly man that God created you to be. Why do you think the devil fights you so hard? He doesn't want you to reach your full potential and start becoming the impactful person God has called you to be.

There is an all-out assault against men in our country right now. We have been marginalized, disregarded, overlooked, and told to be quiet and take a back seat. Society attempts to cancel men from being the influencers that God called us to be. God not only intends for us men to be strong, but he also expects for us to be present.

Senator Josh Hawley, Missouri, called out those who are trying to redefine traditional masculinity as toxic. He is calling for a revival of strong and healthy manhood in America. He said this is an effort that some have been at for years now and they have had alarming success. I want to say that I believe this attack on us is from the devil himself and he uses others to carry out his plan. Hawley goes on to say, "American men are working less, they are getting married in fewer numbers,

---

156. Marcel Schwantes, Inc., "What Separates Successful People From the Pack." August 30, 2022, https://www.inc.com/marcel-schwantes/warren-buffett-says-what-separates-successful-people-from-pack-comes-down-to-one-simple-word.html.

they're fathering fewer children, they're suffering more anxiety and depression, and they're engaging in more substance abuse."[157]

Men are confused and many of us are not handling our business. That's why I wanted to write this book. To encourage you to Man UP and be the strong man that God created you to be. I pray you don't feel beat up after reading this book, but challenged, inspired, and motivated. I'm not trying to bash you or any of us. I've already acknowledged that it's hard work being a man. But we can do this. Please don't disqualify yourself or decide to sit this one out. That's what our enemy wants from us. He knows of the impact that we can have when we walk in the destiny that God has for us. The devil is doing his best to silence us and marginalize our influence for Christ.

I've recently discovered the books of Erwin W. Lutzer, who has quickly become one of my favorite authors. He is an evangelical Christian speaker, radio broadcaster, and former senior pastor of The Moody Church in Chicago, Illinois. Last year I read one of his newest books, *We Will Not be Silenced*, and it stirred up my heart and soul. Lutzer believes we are living in a time where certain groups of people are being told to be quiet about our views and keep our values to ourselves. So, if you are not a part of one of the socially protected tribes–like women, transgender and gay people, or minorities–well, we've heard enough from you, so it's time for you to sit there and not speak. If you happen to be a bit old-fashioned,

---

157. Rachel Treisman, NPR, "Sen. Josh Hawley claims masculinity is under attack," https://www.npr.org/2021/11/11/1054615028/is-masculinity-under-attack-sen-hawley-wants-to-defend-the-men-of-america.

Christian, conservative, or if you are a man—you need to zip it, according to today's culture.

All along, some predators with a wicked agenda are trying to push values and beliefs on our young boys (and girls) that do not line up with what most of us believe. Lutzer points out their goal is clear, "Attack any form of decency, sacredness, or normal sexual relations. Confuse the children by awakening sexual desires reserved for adults, and utterly destroy any concept of the traditional family. Encourage children to have multiple sexual experiences. And in the process, reap the consequences: more abortions, more anti-religious bigotry, and most importantly, more broken homes."[158]

This isn't a new agenda; it's been in the works for a while. Dr. James Dobson took a lot of heat for speaking out against this radical feminist agenda way back in the 80s. Yet, this should show us why it's so important to Man UP and become the godly men that He has called us to be. It's just about us. We are Manning UP so we can help others.

FROM TOXIC MASCULINITY TO NOXIOUS FEMINISM

A few years ago, our society finally acknowledged the routine mistreatment of women and attempted to address the chauvinistic and misogynistic tendencies that have, ashamedly, permeated our societies. We acknowledged that women have been marginalized, overlooked, disrespected, and taken advantage of for years. This mostly happened at the hands of men, who believed women were inferior to them. They were

---

158. Erwin W. Lutzer, *We Will Not Be Silenced* (Eugene, OR: Harvest House Publishers, 2020).

taught to work hard in order to become the alpha male. It was common to think that "boys will be boys" and that a woman's place in our society was to be subservient to the whims of the men in their life. (Would it be too distracting if I made a joke right here? Yeah, I better not). The point is that many men displayed behavior that was toxic towards women. In time, we came to label this behavior as toxic masculinity.

Toxic masculinity refers to the notion that some people's idea of "manliness" perpetuates domination and aggression. Furthermore, it involves cultural pressures for men to behave in a certain way, and claims that we most likely teach boys these negative and destructive tendencies towards women.

After watching our society attempt to course correct, I assert that in our quest to eradicate toxic masculinity, the pendulum has swung all the way over to the other side, we are now experiencing "noxious (dangerous) feminism."

I realize that for decades women were treated less than they should have been in our society and this was damaging to the mindset and outlook for many women, both young and old. Steps needed to be taken to correct this. However, I believe we may have swung the pendulum too far to the other side and, essentially, over corrected. Our culture is prone to emasculate men in our movies, TV shows, homes, businesses, and society at large. This is disappointing.

In reality, there is room for both sexes to be empowered and thrive. However, noxious feminism says that in order for women to thrive, we must degrade men and remove them from positions of power and authority. In essence, in order to make room for women at the table, we have removed men from the table and kicked them out of the room, emasculating them in the process. Have we thought about what this says to our children, both boys and girls?

One of the concerns about toxic masculinity is that it suggests that men need to act tough and avoid showing emotions. This is harmful to their mental health and has serious consequences for society. This is how it became known as "toxic masculinity." I'm not a proponent of teaching this to the next generation of young men. On the flip side, we must also acknowledge that teaching women they can do whatever they want and that they don't need a man for anything is equally destructive to our society. This contributes to the identity crisis that a lot of young girls are having as individuals and members of a social group.

We are painting an unrealistic perspective about life. An overwhelming number of movies are projecting the superheroes as women with superpowers and super strength. We see them battling and defeating larger men in hand-to-hand combat, many of whom also have superpowers and strength. It's unbelievable to the naked eye. It's not realistic for us to project that women are physically better and stronger than men, and can defeat men in every arena. This is just not the case. Men are physically stronger than women; biology has revealed this to be absolutely true. It is what it is. However, that doesn't mean that women are weak.

Women have emotional, physical, and God-given biological strength to reproduce life. Through much pain and agony, women have populated the planet by having babies, which is one of the most awesome displays of strength known to mankind. Let's be honest, men don't have the strength to endure the pain of childbirth like women do. If men had babies, maybe only every other guy might have one. We can't handle pain like women can. Personally, I'm allergic to pain! It makes me break out crying.

It disappoints me that we are telling young girls that they can do everything that a man can do. That is simply not true. Whether we want to admit it or not, collectively, men are physically stronger, more aggressive, prone to roughhousing, and are born with God-given instincts to protect and provide. That's the way God made us. We have a propensity towards and can do things that women can't do. To say that women can't do everything that men can do doesn't infer that I believe men are better than women. I don't believe that. We are just different. Therefore, we should acknowledge this and work at being complementary and supportive of each other just as God intended.

As kids, we were introduced to concepts like the battle of the sexes. Further evaluation would indicate this is harmful and destructive towards teaching our children how to have a proper relationship with members of the opposite sex. Men and women don't need to compete with each other. Instead, we should support and complement each other. Instead of teaching young girls they can do everything boys can do, I propose we start teaching young girls that they can do everything that God says they can do. The same is true for our young boys; they can do everything that God says they can do. When our boys and girls are listening to what God says, they will realize that we need mutual respect, honor, and appreciation of both sexes. This is totally opposite of what they are seeing now…each sex demeaning, denigrating, disparaging, and devaluing the other one. That's not cool–and very destructive for our society!

The truth is, men and women are interdependent upon each other. We were made to go together and we need each other. Let's work together to rid our relationships of both toxic masculinity and noxious feminism. I encourage us to consider the words of Paul, that he wrote in the Book of Hebrews when he encouraged us to think of ways to motivate one another to acts of love and good works.[159] He challenged us to encourage each other every day. This is a far cry from spreading toxic and noxious behavior.

THE STAKES ARE HIGH

Men, we need you to start engaging and leading so that we can redeem our culture. Don't let anyone tell you that our society doesn't need strong men, because they do. There are too many boys growing up without positive role models. Remember, it takes a man to show a man how to be a man. Your community needs you. Your children need you. Your wife needs you to be a strong man. We need men whose lives are above reproach; men who are faithful to their wives. Men who exercise self-control, live wisely, and have a good reputation.[160] That's how Paul encouraged the leaders of the Early Church to be–and that's what I'm encouraging you to strive for.

But, let's be real; no leader wants to be a fraud, a pretender, a hypocrite. That's why some of you are waiting or holding

---

159. Hebrews 10:24–25.
160. 1 Timothy 3:2.

back. I get it. But, it's time. In fact, it's past time. The stakes are way too high for us to wait to be perfect before we decide to engage. That's not what I'm asking and that's not what God's asking.

You don't need to be perfect or without fault. You only need to be committed. Committed to taking David's advice to be strong, act like a man, and observe what the Lord requires: walk in obedience to Him, and keep His commands. Do this so that you may prosper in all you do and wherever you go. It's time. Man UP!

Contact Alex at Alex@AlexBryant.org
Website is AlexBryant.org

Other books by Alex
Let's Start Again: A Biracial Couples View on Race, Racial Ignorance, and Racial Insensitivity